How to Draw Anime Girls

A Step-by-Step Guide for Kids, Teens and Adult

SHINJUKU PRESS

Thank you for getting our book!

If you find this drawing book fun and useful, we would be very grateful if you post a short review on Amazon! Your support does make a difference and we read every review personally.

If you would like to leave a review, just head on over to this book's Amazon page and click "Write a customer review".

Thank you for your support!

Contents

Introduction

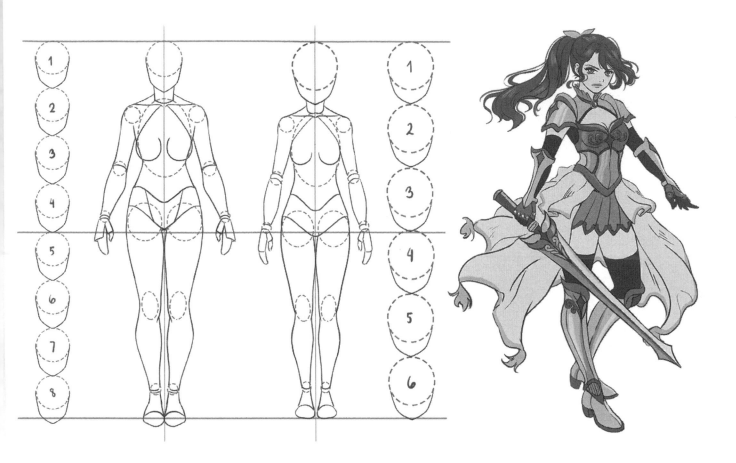

Are you among the millions of people worldwide who are really into anime? As you watch anime, do you feel an inner passion or perhaps you like the characters a lot and want to recreate them yourself? And maybe, these characters stir up an urge to even create your own world from imagination.

Suppose that you draw the characters that you love but you aren't too happy with them. The proportions aren't quite right, the bodies may look rigid, or you just don't know where to start! Now, you are left feeling frustrated and lost.

Rest assured, anyone can learn how to draw anime characters. It's fun, and although technical at times, it's fairly simple when the steps are broken down beginning with learning the foundation. Once you've grasped that, drawing a face, body, and even clothing should be much easier. Also, when you are familiar with the foundation, you likely can see the characters in your head help you draw from your imagination.

In this guide book, you will learn how to draw anime girls: their heads from any angle with facial features, different body types, and assorted clothes. Lastly, you will be drawing assorted characters that will inspire you toward creating your very own characters.

The lessons are aimed at people who want to draw anime girls. The goal is for you to improve your drawing skills with the help of an artist who began much like you. Someone who is a fan of anime and began drawing without knowing the foundation. Eventually, I discovered that I was actually doing it wrong the whole time. Then I began to study technical drawings of human figures. Even though anime is different from realistic drawings, the characters possess the same components. To simplify a drawing into an anime style, you must know why something is the way it is.

Together, let's go on a journey to refine the quality of your anime drawing with a fun patient-driven approach to ensure success!

Faces

DRAWING A GIRL – FRONT VIEW

1. Draw a circle. Try to make it as round as you can.

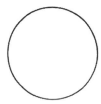

2. Find the center of the circle. Draw a horizontal and a vertical line through the center with the endpoints on the circle.

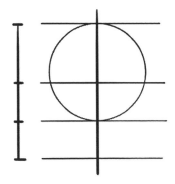

3. Slightly below the eyebrow is where you'll find the eyes. The mouth is in-between the nose and chin. Draw the outline of the face and add the neck.

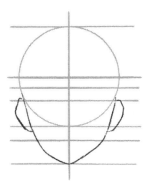

4.   Add the facial features. The top of the ear aligns with the top of the eyes while the bottom aligns with the nose.

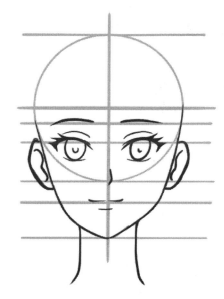

5.   Draw the outline of the hair and add some lines where you want the hair to go.

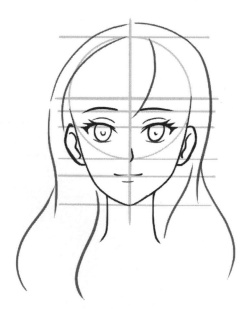

6. Add details to the hair. Think of the hair as wide, heavy ribbons instead of individual strands.

7. Clean your lines and erase the guidelines.

8. Finally, it's time to shade. Be mindful of where your light source is to help you know where to put the shadows. Since girls have softer features, make your shading light and soft. And you're done!

DRAWING A GIRL – SIDE VIEW

1. Draw a circle and a curved line to the side. This will be the front of the head.

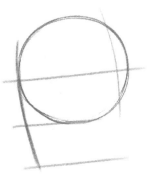

2. Draw a slightly slanted line across the middle of the circle. Just like in the front view, all the lines are equal in distance.

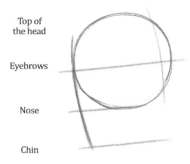

3. Add a line near the edge of the circle to place the ear. Start drawing the outline of the head and the ear.

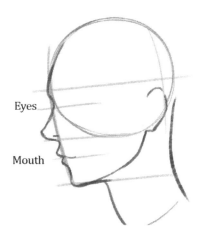

4. To draw the eye, think of it like a triangle since it is facing the front and is covered by the eyelids. Also, draw the mouth.

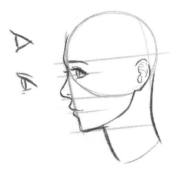

5. The head is big so make sure you keep that in mind when you add the hair. The ear can be your guide because it is in the middle between the front and back of the head.

6. Add some details on the hair and erase what will be hidden underneath the hair.

7. Do some final touch ups like erasing the guidelines.

8. You may choose to shade your drawing. And you're done!

DRAWING A GIRL – ¾ VIEW

1. Start with a circle and make a curved center line. The curve is to show the roundness of the head.

2. Divide the circle in half and then add another line below the circle, the same distance apart.

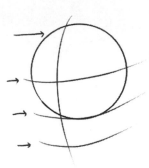

3. Draw the outline of the face including the ear and the neck. Remember that we will see more of the jaw from this angle.

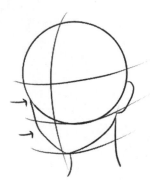

4. Draw the eyes, nose, and mouth. Follow the shapes of the eyes.

5. Design what kind of hairstyle you want your character to have.

6. Create more lines for details.

7. Erase the guidelines. You may use a pen to create cleaner lines.

8. You may also choose to shade or color your finished line art drawing. And you're done!

How to Draw Anime Girl Eyes

When drawing the facial features, I always start with the eyes. This style is semi-realistic.

1. Draw the outline that you learned from drawing the head in the front view. It should have a center line. Usually, the distance between the eyes is roughly the length of one eye.

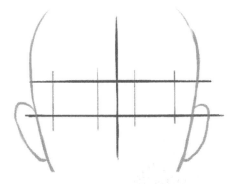

2. It is important to draw the outline of the eyes first before you add details. This way, your drawing will have a good foundation.

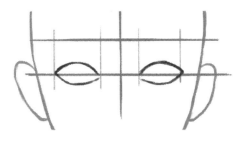

3. Proceed to add the iris and pupil of each eye. For this example, the girl is looking directly at us so the iris will look like a half-circle.

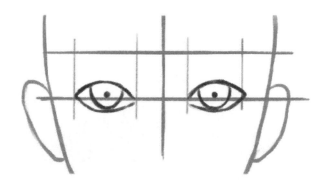

4. Draw the eyelids and the eyebrows.

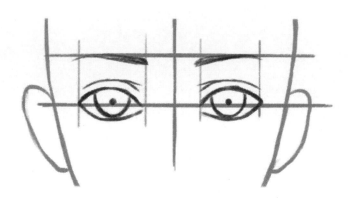

5. Erase the guidelines and make some adjustments such as adding the eyelashes or the highlight and making your lines clean. And you're done!

How to Draw Anime Girl Eyes – Version 2

You will also learn how to draw in this style. It has more of a classic anime look.

1. For this type of eyes, the outline will be much bigger and placed lower on the face than in the first example. The shape of the head is also much rounder.

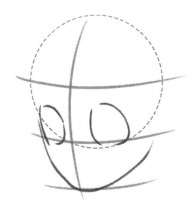

2. Next, draw some thicker lines on the upper part of the eyes. Be mindful of the angle.

3. Add the irises, eyebrows, and eyelashes.

4. You can be as fancy as you want with details.

5. Clean up your lines and do some adjustments for a more polished look. Since the eyes are already big enough, make the nose and mouth tiny. And you're done!

EXAMPLES OF ANIME GIRL EYES

I will show you how to draw eyes in different styles and emotions.

Default/Happy Eyes:

For this type of eyes, the eyebrows are usually relaxed.

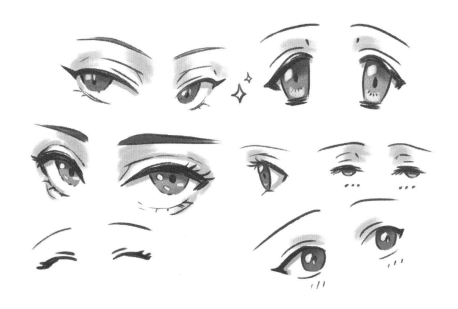

Surprised Eyes:

To show surprise, the iris will be a lot smaller depending on how surprised the character is.

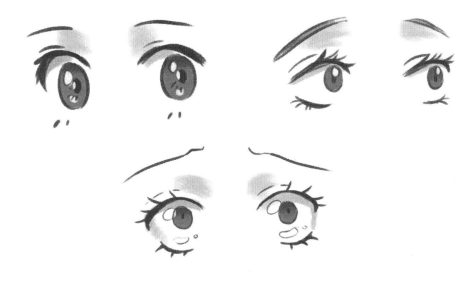

Upset Eyes:

To show agitation, the eyebrows are drawn going upward. Sometimes, there will be a crease on the forehead.

Worried Eyes:

While the eyebrows go upward to show upset eyes, they are drawn the opposite to show worry.

How to Draw Anime Girl Noses

The next facial feature that you will draw is the nose. This is the easiest part to draw, depending on the style that you choose.

1. First, draw your guidelines and the shape of the head.

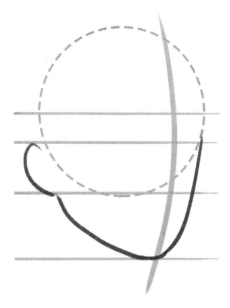

2. Then draw the bridge of the nose. It usually looks like a curved line in anime.

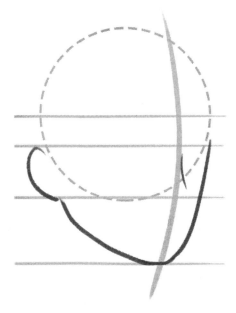

3. Draw another curved line at an angle.

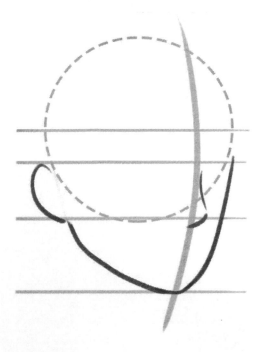

4. This type of nose may look finished but you can add a nostril if you prefer. Then, you're done!

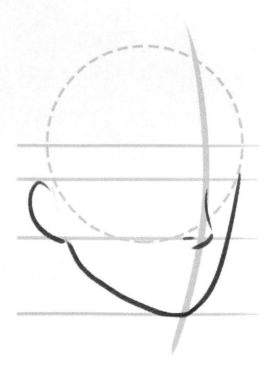

5. There's also another type of nose that is very angular and also easy to draw.

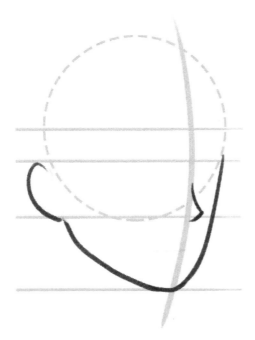

6. A different type looks like a backward "L".

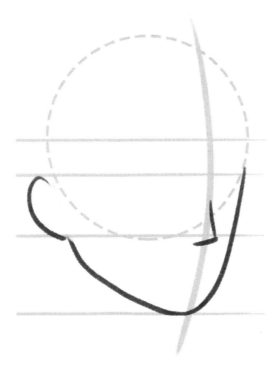

Examples:

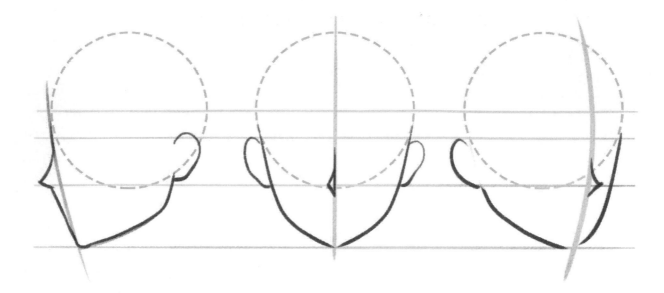

For the front view, you just have to draw a straight line and add a tiny triangle.

EXAMPLES OF ANIME GIRL NOSES

Let's look at a few other types of noses that you can draw.

Examples:

You will notice that this type is semi-realism. The ball of the nose and the nostrils are more defined.

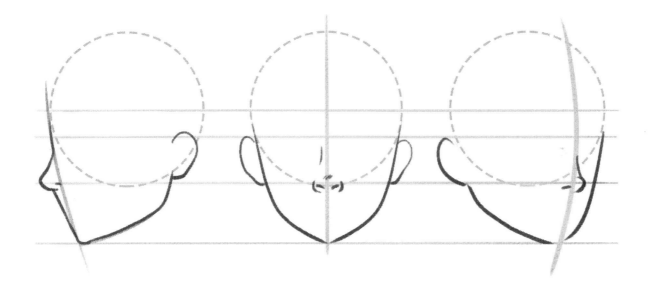

These examples show the outline of the nose from different angles.

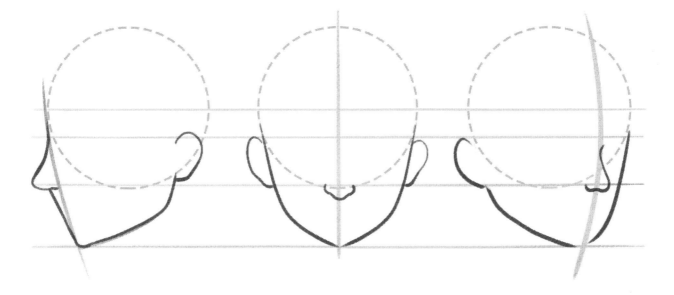

More examples:

The first one only shows the nostrils. The second one has a dot and the last draws the shape of the nose and the shadow.

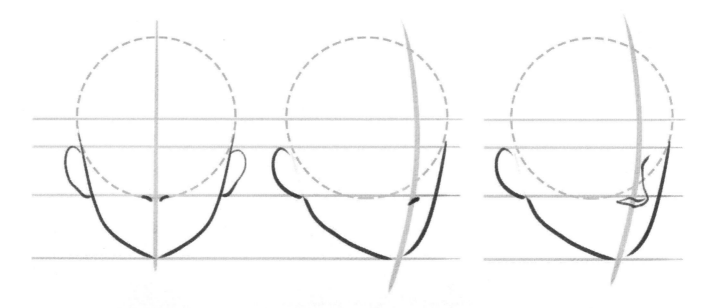

How to Draw Anime Girl Mouths

The last facial feature to draw is the mouth. It is also very simple.

1.   As usual, establish your guidelines and foundation.

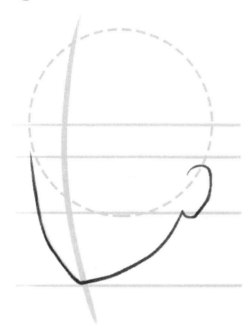

2.   For this example, we will draw lips that are slightly smiling. First, draw a straight line in-between the bottom of the nose and the chin.

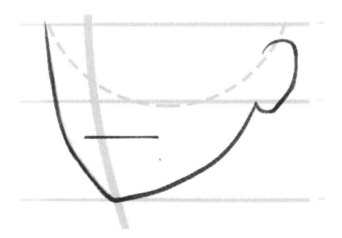

3. Add a small dot to both ends of the line. Then add a small "V" shape in the middle. Since this is a ³/₄ view, the "V" will be a bit distorted.

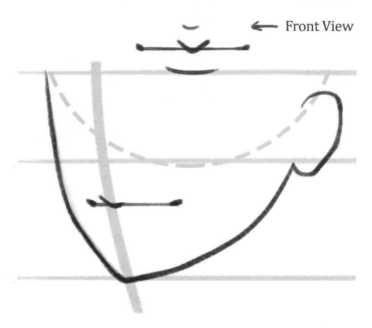

Front View

4. Erase a little of the straight line. Then draw a curved line starting from the "V" shape and meeting the edge of the lips similar to a mustache!

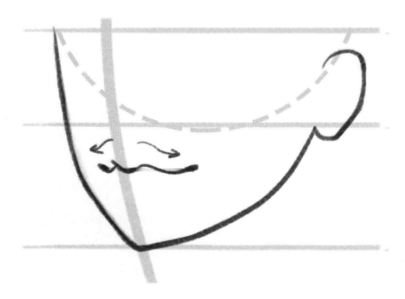

5. The last thing to draw are the upper and bottom lips.

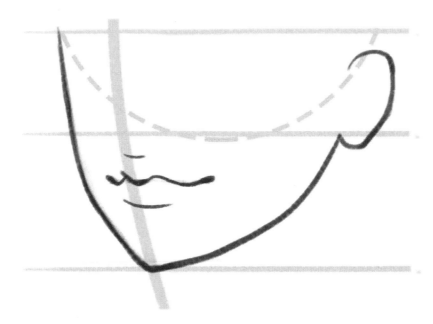

6. You can also shade the lips but keep in mind that if your character is wearing lipstick, you should use a darker color.

Examples:

Some anime lips are very simple like these. I recommend using them on characters with big eyes. That way the lips wouldn't be as distracting if you want the viewers to focus on the eyes.

Most of the time, these types of lips are used for younger characters.

EXAMPLES OF ANIME MOUTHS

Let's now learn about the different emotions that the mouth can show. Each emotion is drawn differently.

Happy:

Here are some examples of uplifted reactions. Sometimes the teeth and tongue are drawn to show a character with a happy expression.

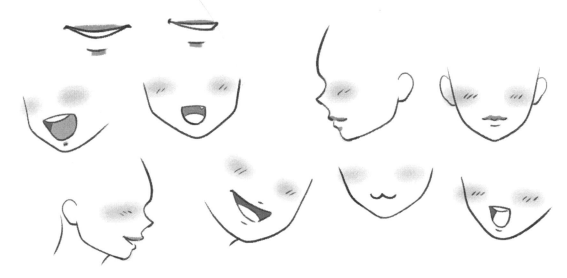

Sad/Upset:

To express someone being sad or upset, make sure to emphasize the downward curve.

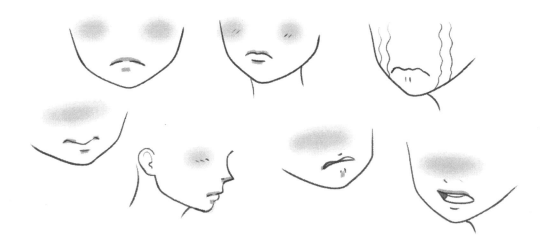

Talking:

There are many ways to draw someone talking. You can choose your preference from these examples:

Shouting:

When you draw someone shouting, make the mouth as big as you can. Keep in mind that the head sometimes expands because the jaw opens wider.

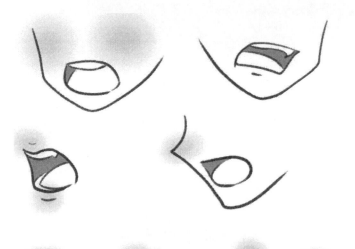

Mischievous:

For a mischievous expression, the edges of the mouth are curved up and/or the tongue is out to show teasing.

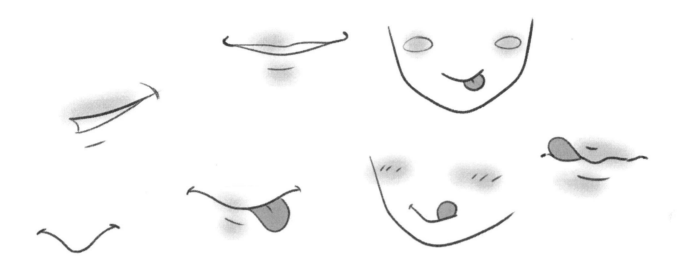

TIPS ON HOW TO DRAW ANIME HAIR

There are many tips to help you succeed in designing your character's hair.

1. Volume

Hair has volume. Think of hair in groups or by sections. You can add extra strands later if you want but the most important thing is that you've established the weight and volume of the hair.

2. Silhouette

One question to ask yourself is: "Does the hair have a good silhouette?" If your design has good shapes, it will be more interesting to look at. Also, it is much easier to fill in when you have an initial silhouette.

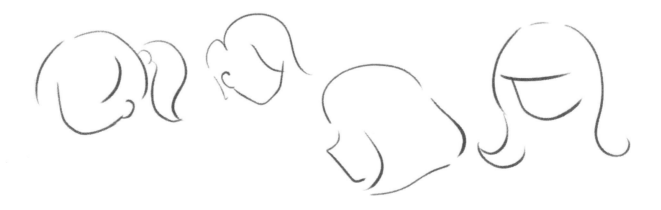

3.   Direction

Every section of the hair has an origin. Always keep in mind the origin.

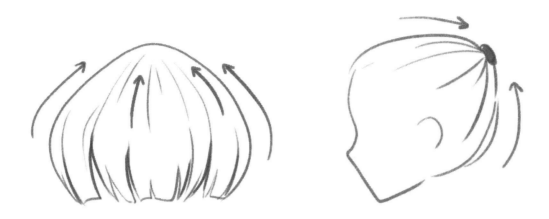

There are a few more tips that you must know to further understand the logic behind the complex anatomy of hair.

4.   Avoid "Spaghetti Hair"

We know that hair has volume but we should not rule out that hair is still made out of individual strands. So, what is spaghetti hair? It's when the hair is drawn in hair strands.

This may be the style you are going for but it presents a hollow feeling because it doesn't have the right foundation for the hair to sit on top of.

To solve this problem, simply divide the hair into sections or parts. This way, you will give the hair the necessary weight and volume.

5.   Matching a Hairstyle to Your Character
There are tons of hairstyles to choose from, so how do you know what kind you should give to your character?

When designing a character, it's important to consider the character's personality. That way, it will be easier to reflect their personality on choices of clothing, accessories, and even hairstyle.

For example, let's take a look at this character.

When you look at her, you get the impression that she may be childish or that she has a bubbly personality. For all we know, she could be an adult.

I intentionally made her hair more rounded because round or curved lines represent the positive/happy energy around us like ocean waves.

The ocean is seen with curvy waves when it is calm. But when there's a storm, the waves are pointy and more aggressive.

Remember that when you design your character's hair.

More Tips on Deciding Hairstyle

The Shy Hairstyle

The next character that we're going to look at is the shy type.

We can immediately tell that she is a shy type because there's hair that is covering half of her face.

Covering the face this much also creates a mysterious aura.

Deciding what kind of expression and pose to give your character will also tell the personality that you are going for.

Lastly, the design of the eyes also plays a huge part on the character design since it's the first thing that people usually look at.

The Extroverted Hairstyle

For an extroverted hairstyle, you can use some spiky lines to show that the character has a determined/bold persona.

Just like the pointier, aggressive ocean waves, the spiky lines reflect the character's straightforward personality.

Usually, a spiky hairstyle is used in popular Shounen anime that is geared toward teenage boys and features a male protagonist who embarks on an adventure filled with challenges.

Studying your favorite anime characters can help give you ideas of different hairstyle designs for your own drawings.

COMMON TYPES OF BANGS

Let's start with the most common types of bangs.

Straight bangs

First, draw the silhouette then add sections of hair that will eventually point to the origin. Next, add more details and then clean up the rest.

One-Sided bangs

The process of drawing this type is similar to drawing straight bangs.

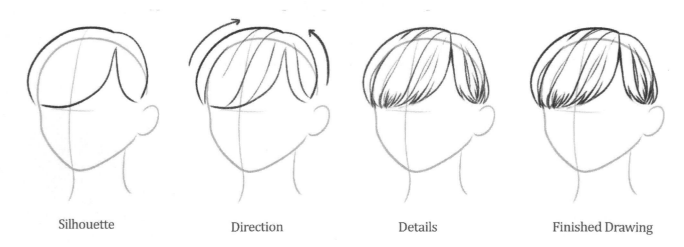

Silhouette   Direction   Details   Finished Drawing

Middle-parted bangs

Usually, this style wraps around the head. Drawing this way will give the hair lots of volume and depth.

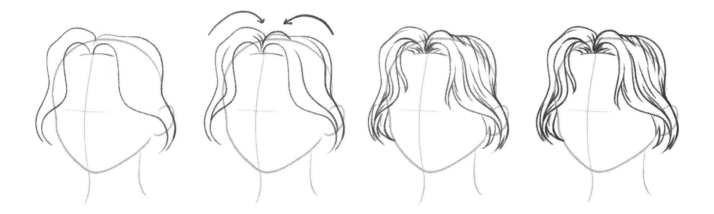

Different Types of Bangs

Now, there are many ways to draw the bangs. It's your choice how you want your character to look. Here are a few examples.

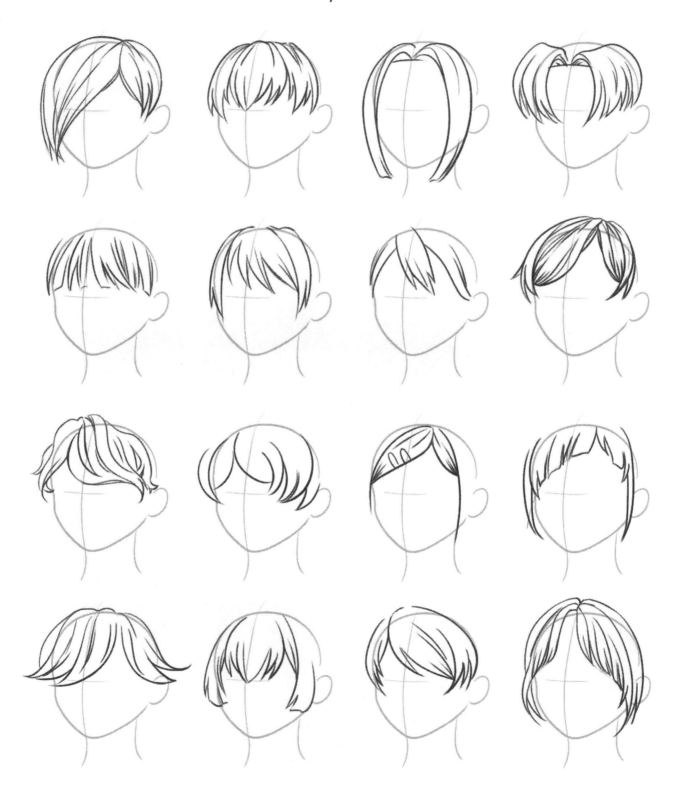

HOW TO DRAW LONG HAIR

Now that we know the tips and tricks behind designing hair, we can move on to the process of drawing long hair.

1. As usual, start with an overall shape or silhouette of the design that you want.

2. Decide what type of bangs for your character then draw the lines that point back to the origin.

3. Add details and also keep in mind that the hair is divided in sections. Only add small details at the end of the sections and the edges.

4. Add some overlapping hair to give the hair some depth and provide interest. Polish up and you're done!

HAIRSTYLE EXAMPLES – LONG AND TIED

HOW TO DRAW SHORT HAIR

The next hairstyle we will tackle is short hair. This type of hairstyle is another choice to describe the personality of the character that you are making.

1.   Start designing the silhouette of the character.

2.   Divide the hair into sections to help make the style.

3. Since the hairstyle of this character is somewhat wavy, make sure you curl up the sections of hair.

4. Add a headband for a cute finishing touch and you're done!

How to Draw a Pigtail Hairstyle

One of the most common hairstyles is also a pigtail so let's learn how to draw this style for your character.

1.   Pick what type of bangs for your character before you draw the silhouette of the pigtails. For this example, we will learn how to draw braids.

2.   Proceed to divide the sections on the bangs and then find the centerline of the cylinder shapes of the braids. Draw them in relation to the perspective.

3. To draw the braids, think of them like drawing stairs but they gradually get smaller as you go down.

Don't align the curves

4. Erase the centerline a little as you add more details to the hair. The shape of the braid should look like fluffy stairs.

5. The last thing to do is to erase the guidelines and make the line art neat. And you're done!

Funky Hairstyle Examples

Different Head Shapes

There are many different ways to draw the shape of the head in the anime style.

Common Head Shape

This is the type of head that you will often see in most anime art styles where the chin is pointy.

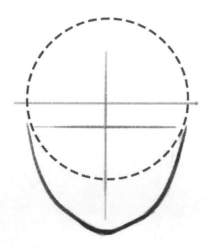

Oval Head

It is similar to a round face but just somewhat elongated to represent an oval shape.

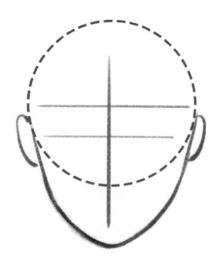

Semi-Realistic Head

For this type of head, the chin is flatter and more defined like in real-life.

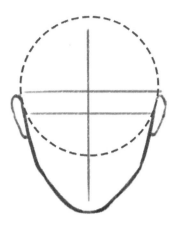

Square Jaw

This type of head is very angular especially where the jaw connects to the chin.

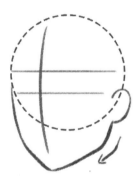

Round Head

To achieve this look, just simply make the jaw smoother and more circular.

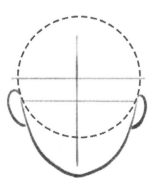

Diamond Head

This is similar to the square jaw where it is angular but eventually leads to a pointed chin.

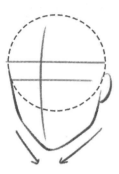

Heart Shape

The heart shape is when the cheekbone is more pronounced and the chin is pointy. You will also see a widow's peak on the hairline that completes the heart shape.

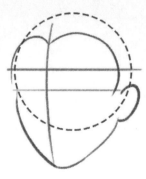

Rectangle Head

This type is also similar to the square jaw where the head is longer in length but boxier.

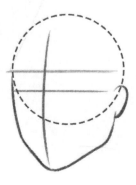

Makeup Tutorial for Girls

Adding makeup can really magnify the design aspect of your character especially their eyes. There are a few ways to really pop the eyes and overall aesthetic of the face.

1.   Draw a basic face with facial features. Add a hairstyle if you want.

2.   Draw an outline at $1/3$ corner of the eye. This is the part where you can be creative with the shape.

3. Fill in the outline by shading inside. You will also shade the mouth for lipstick.

4. Define the eyelids more by shading the overall shape. Keep it subtle like smokey eyeshadows.

5. Add some eyelashes or mascara to the eyes. Randomize the thickness of the eyelashes for a more natural look.

6. Lastly, modify the lipstick more by making the upper lip darker and adding a highlight on the bottom lip. Don't forget the blush!

Different Eye Makeup:

Simple eyeshadow
and eyeliner

Double flick eyeliner

Full eyelashes

Extra-thick eyeliner

A Fun Makeup Tutorial

Maybe you want something fun for the makeup or you might have an unusual character that you want to bring to life. Adding crazy and fun makeup can help with that.

1. As usual, draw a basic face with facial features. Since we're making an unusual character, pick an expression that is unique.

2. Design the type of makeup that will match the character's personality. In this example, the star shape suits the expression that she's making.

3. Fill in the shapes with black and include the eyeliner.

4. Next, shade in some lipstick. Don't forget to make the upper lip darker.

5. And finally, add some blush on the middle of her face. And you're done!

BODIES

TIPS ON HOW TO DRAW THE FEMALE BODY

The body figure is such a complex organic matter but there are methods where we can break it down to manageable shapes. You will also learn some tips and tricks to successfully establish your foundation where the body sits.

1.   Measurements

As you probably can tell, drawing the body is very technical but don't let that intimidate you. As soon as you get the hang of it, you'll be able to draw from your imagination without even using the guidelines.

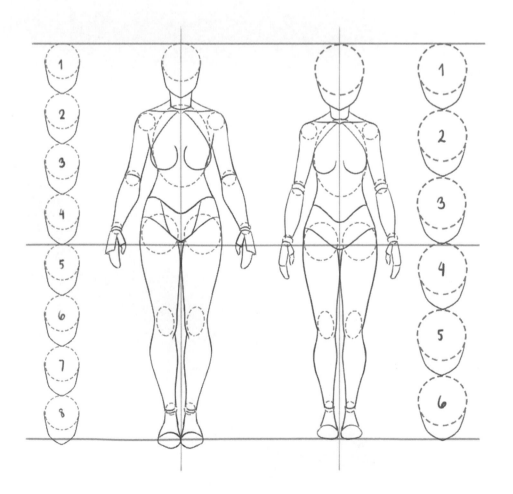

Measuring the height of the character is quite easy. You just measure the height of the head and then multiply it by eight to get the full height. The crotch is usually in the middle.

The same method applies to big-headed characters. The only difference is that there are less heads to stack (e.g., approximately six rather than eight).

However, it still depends on what type of character you're drawing. There are some characters who have longer legs so you need to modify this method.

2. Geometric Shapes

Everyone can draw the basic 2-D geometric shapes: the sphere, cylinder, and square. But it is be more challenging to draw them in perspective (3-D). Drawing this way will help you improve your character designs tremendously as the human figure is made out of mostly geometric shapes.

The Upper Torso

The torso is drawn starting from drawing the ribcage which looks like an egg or oblong shape. From there, you draw two small spheres for the shoulders after you find the centerline. The last thing to add is the collarbone. You combine all of them to create a vest-looking shape.

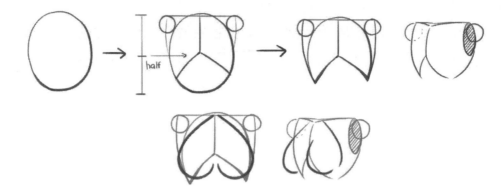

To draw the chest from the front view, think of an upside-down heart where the point connects to the collarbone.

For a 3/4 view, think of a teardrop shape. The size will vary for every female.

The Hips

You can think of the hips like a cylinder but the top is a bit smaller than the bottom. In general, females have wider hips than males but females have smaller ribcages. When you draw the ribcage, make sure it is smaller in width than the hips.

From a cylinder, find the centerline and then start drawing an underwear shape on top of it. This is the perfect shape to also attach the legs where we will put the sphere joints.

3. Gesture Drawing

Once you get the hang of drawing the poses in a stickman or skeleton form, you can move on to adding gestures to your poses. Gesture drawing is the act of capturing the rhythm or feel of the pose to tell a story to the viewer. Being able to capture this is a great skill for an artist because it makes the drawings more visually pleasing.

The gesture can be simplified to straight lines, C or S curves, or a combination. To do gesture drawing, choose among the three that has the closest rhythm to the pose you are trying to capture.

The Arms and Legs

We can draw the arms and legs by combining cylinders and spheres. For the knees, you can use an oval shape. Remember to draw the shapes in perspective.

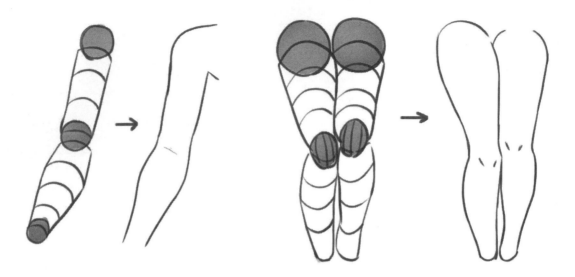

The Hands and Feet

The same goes for the hands and feet. Females have more slender hands than males. Make sure to also follow the rhythm on the tip of the fingers. For the feet, use triangle and rectangle shapes to connect them like a puzzle.

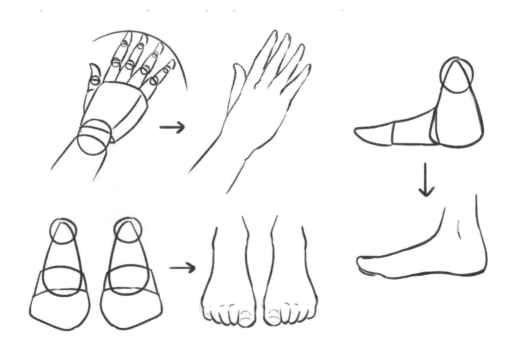

How to Draw the Female Body – Front View

Now that you have the basic understanding of the body, it's time to put every-thing together.

1. We will start by making a straight line vertically using a ruler. This will determine the height. After that, divide the line in half to find the crotch.
2. Draw a skeleton figure. Then draw the collarbone before you draw the arms. Each collarbone is angled up and has roughly the same width as the width of the head.
3. Draw an oval ribcage that is about 1 $\frac{1}{2}$ the height of the head.
4. For the hip bone, draw a cylinder for a good base so it will be easier to convert it into an underwear shape later.

The body width is about the same width as two heads.

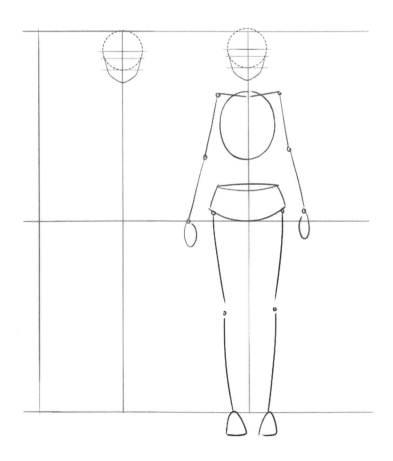

5. Begin drawing some spheres for the joints but use some ovals for the knees. For the shoulder joints, make sure they touch the ribcage.

For the joints on the legs, draw half of them inside the cylinder hip bone.

6. Now that you have the spheres, begin drawing the cylinders for the arms and legs. It's like connecting dots.

Add another cylinder for the neck.

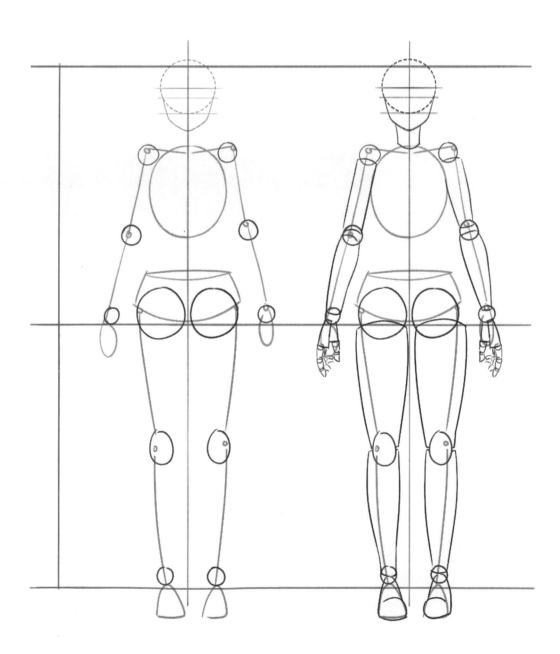

Then draw the boxy shape of the hands.

7.   Erase the skeleton sketch of the arms and legs so it will not be confusing with all the lines that we are adding on top.

It's time to draw the underwear shape as well as add the heart shape on the chest.

After that, connect the ribcage to the hip bone.

8.   Draw the outline of the figure. Remember that females have small waists so make a curve connecting the ribs and the hip bone.

Also, half of the arm aligns with the waist while the hands align with the crotch in a neutral pose like this.

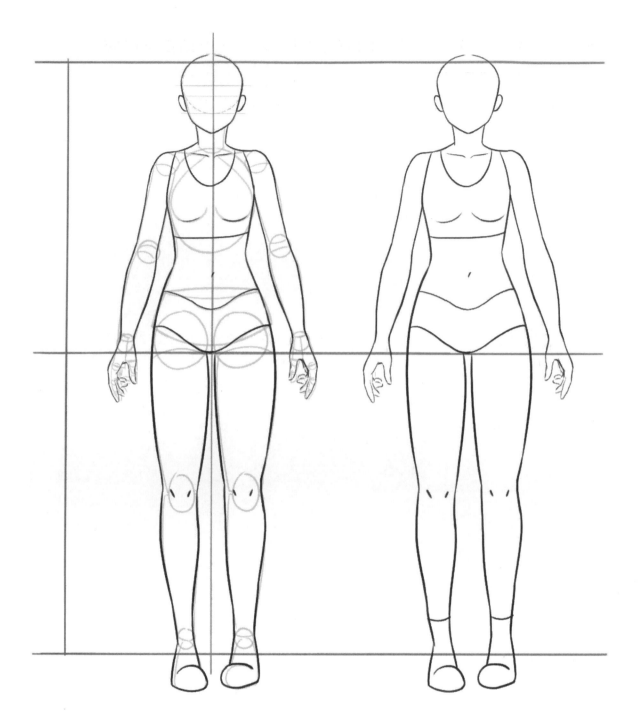

9. Erase the guidelines underneath. You can place the navel just in-between the ribcage and the hip bone.

10. Make some final adjustments like outlining your sketch with a pen. And you're done!

How to Draw the Female Body – Side View

Let's now move on to drawing the human figure from the side view.

1. Establish your lines again like in the front view for proper measurements.
2. We will modify the skeleton a little bit. It will be better to follow the rhythm of the spinal cord because it's easier to place the ribcage and the hip bone.
3. Just follow the rhythm of the spinal cord; the ribcage will appear like it is tilting backwards.

Also note that the hip bone is tilting forward in a neutral position. Make sure you establish the tilted ribcage and the tilted hip bone.

4. For the legs, they also have an S rhythm to them.

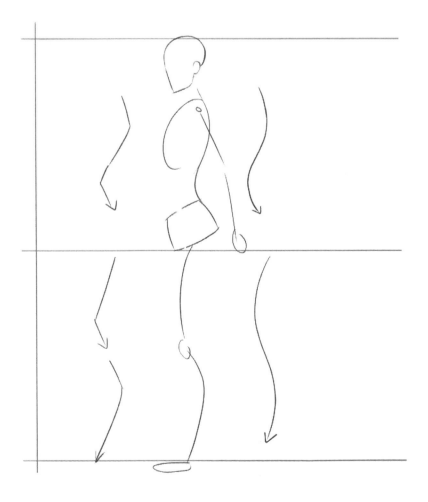

5. Place the spheres for the joints.

6. Now draw the cylinders for the limbs. Draw the other leg but just a little because of this angle.

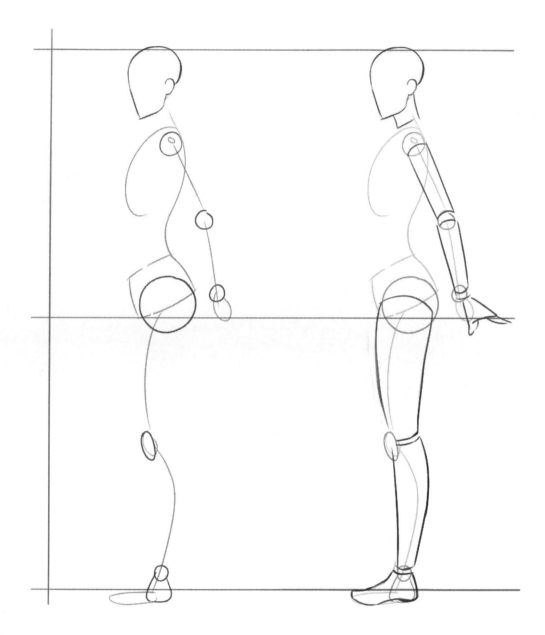

7. To draw the chest in the side view, just draw a teardrop shape but make it a bit flat on the top.

8. In the side view, the underwear is different. It looks somewhat like a crescent moon as it wraps around the leg.

Connect the ribcage to the hip bone. Just below the breast is the ribcage so draw a little bump there. And there's another bump on the lower belly because there are many layers of muscles here.

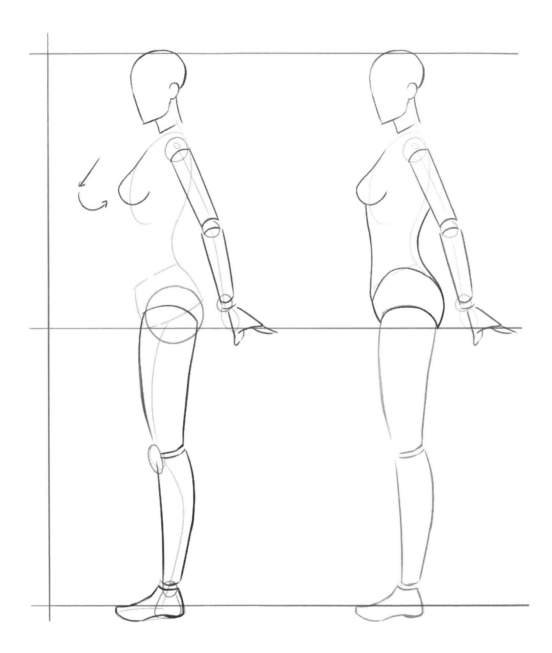

9. Now, it's time for outlining your sketch.
10. Clean up the lines and you're done!

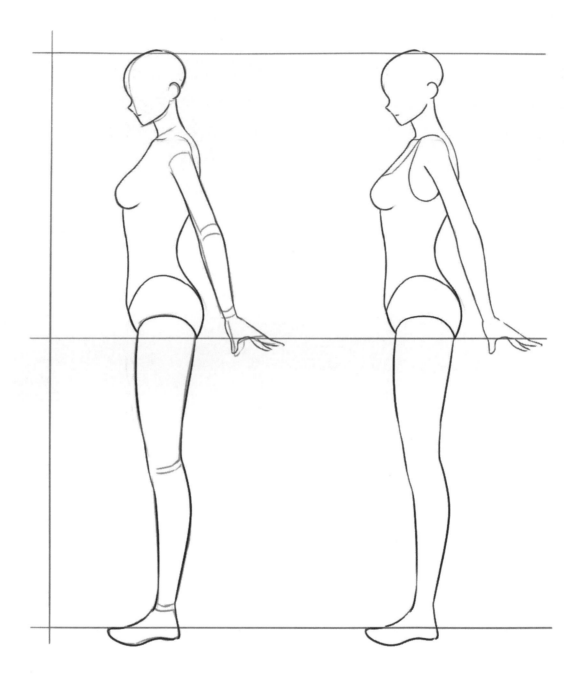

How to Draw the Female Body – 3/4 View

Drawing the body from a three quarter view is very similar to the front view drawing process. You just have to add the volume of the body.

1. To start, draw an oval for the head and then the angle of the shoulder and the hips. It's also nice to add a centerline for the ribcage and hips.
2. Draw the arms and the legs of the skeleton. Then draw the ribcage and the hip bone as a cylinder.

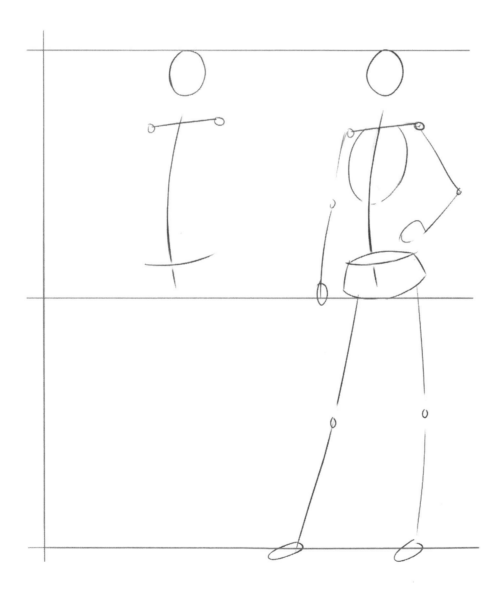

3. Draw the circular joints for each arm and leg. Draw an oval for the knee.

4. Connect the joints with cylinders. Draw them in perspective, too.

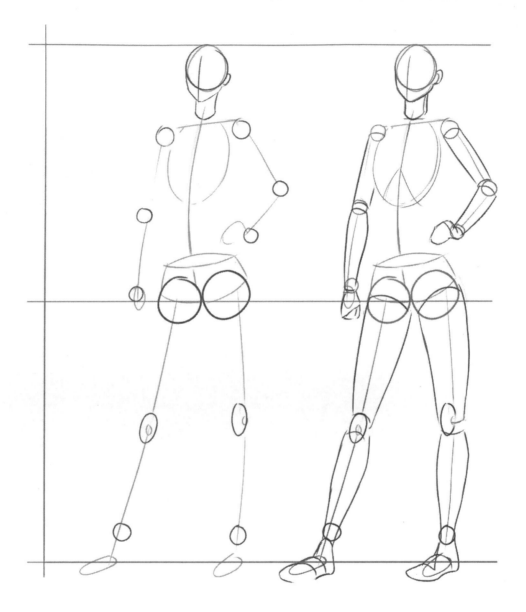

5. Draw the breasts and then draw the connecting curves from the ribcage to the hip bone.

Remember that the breast will look a bit flat on the top because of gravity.

6. Lastly, draw the outline and erase the remaining guidelines underneath. You're done!

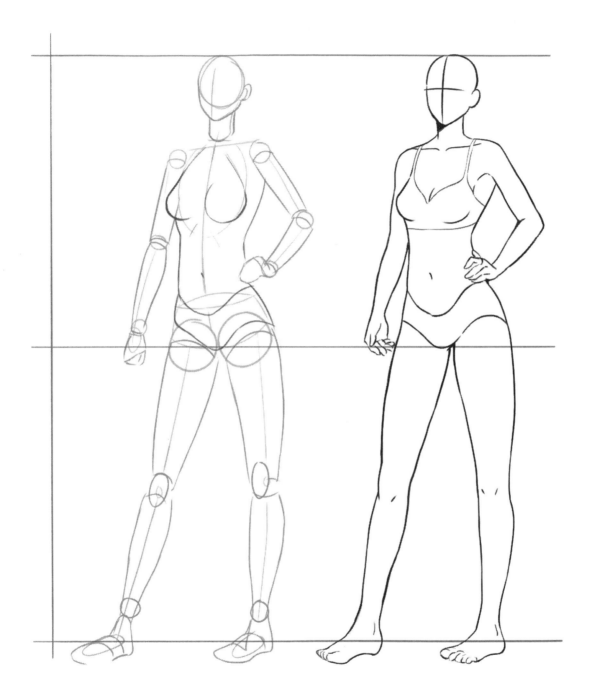

DIFFERENT BODY TYPES

1.   The Standard Type

This body type is where you will use the 8 heads-measurement. It is also the typical body proportions and bodyweight for most women.

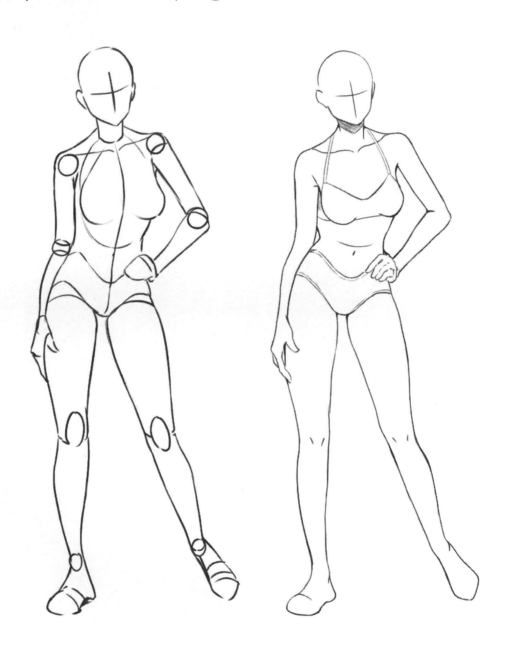

2.   The Curvy Type

The curvy body type has an hourglass figure so make sure you make that prominent. To do so, just draw the hips wider and the thighs thicker. Also, the breasts will be bigger than normal.

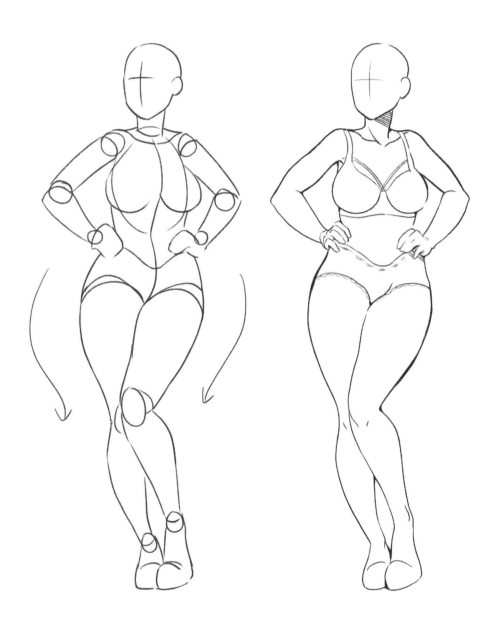

3.   The Athletic Type

Since athletes are physically active, their body muscles will be more developed and leaner. It will be better if you learn some anatomy to be able to draw an athletic body because then you will know the types of muscles that are visible on the surface.

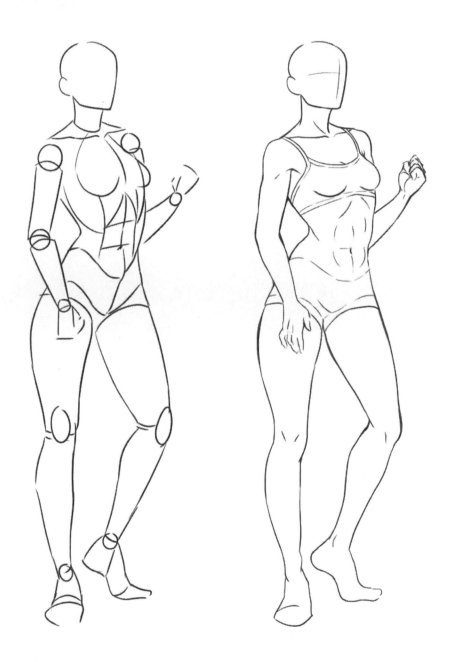

For a woman, don't make the muscles too extreme because the body might end up looking more masculine. However, the style depends on your preference.

4.   The Petite Type

A petite body will have a less curvy waist and hips since the muscles are not as developed. The end result makes the torso look rectangular. You can even draw the torso as a rectangle.

This body usually has smaller breasts and more prominent bones.

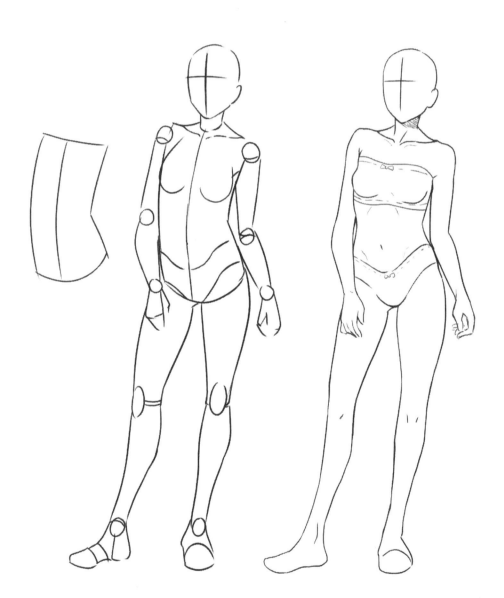

5.   The Plus-Size Body Type

This body type is very similar to the curvy type in terms of the hourglass figure. The only difference is that in plus-size bodies, there are more bumps along the lower belly since this is where the excess weight generally accumulates. Also, since women have wider hips than men, the excess weight will also gather on the thighs but not so much on the lower legs.

These drawings will also have rounder arms and bigger breasts.

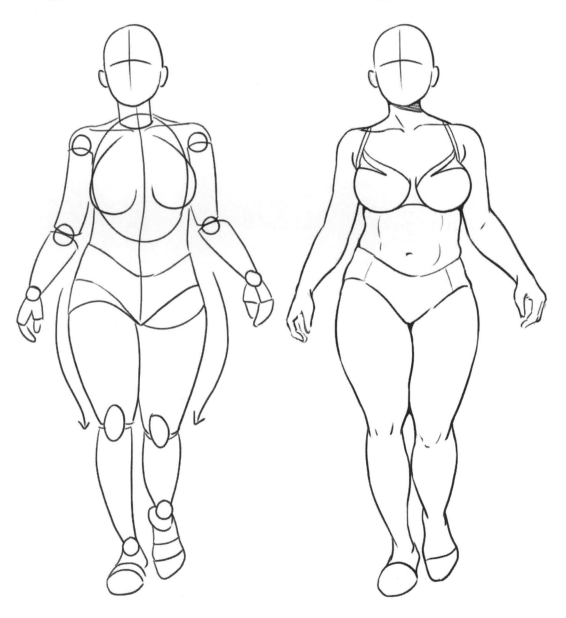

Poses – Examples for Practice

1. Typical Anime Poses

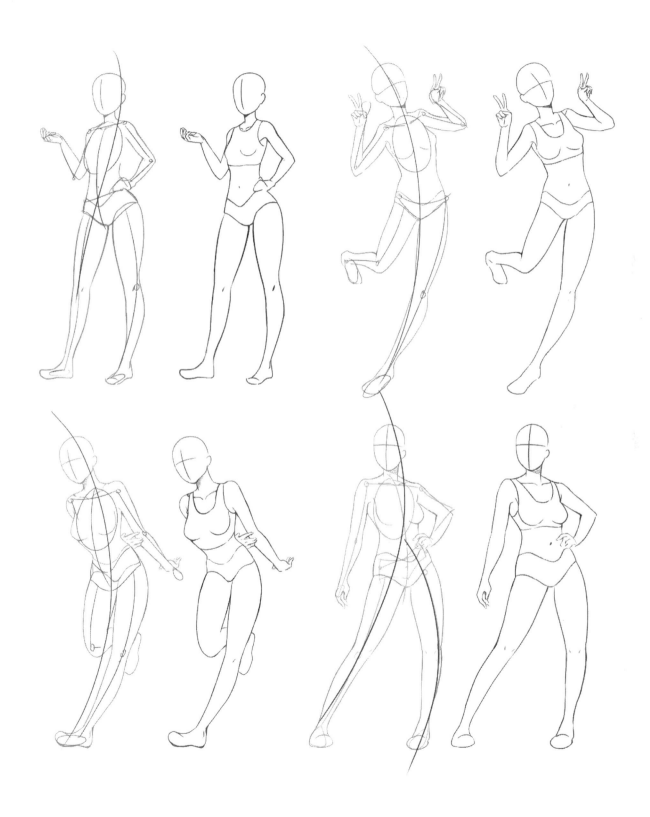

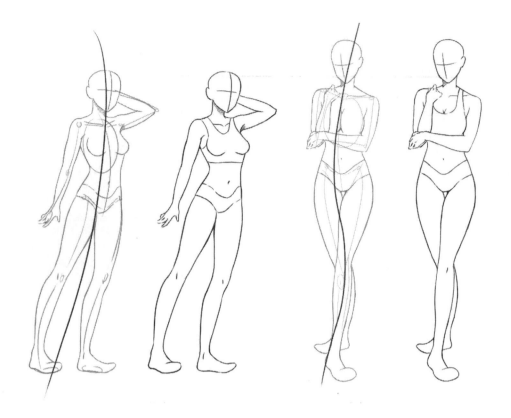

2. Sitting Poses

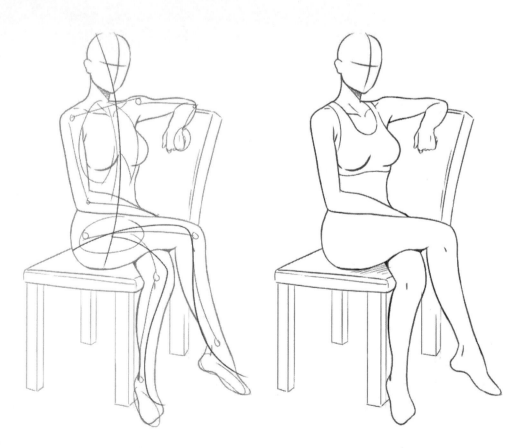

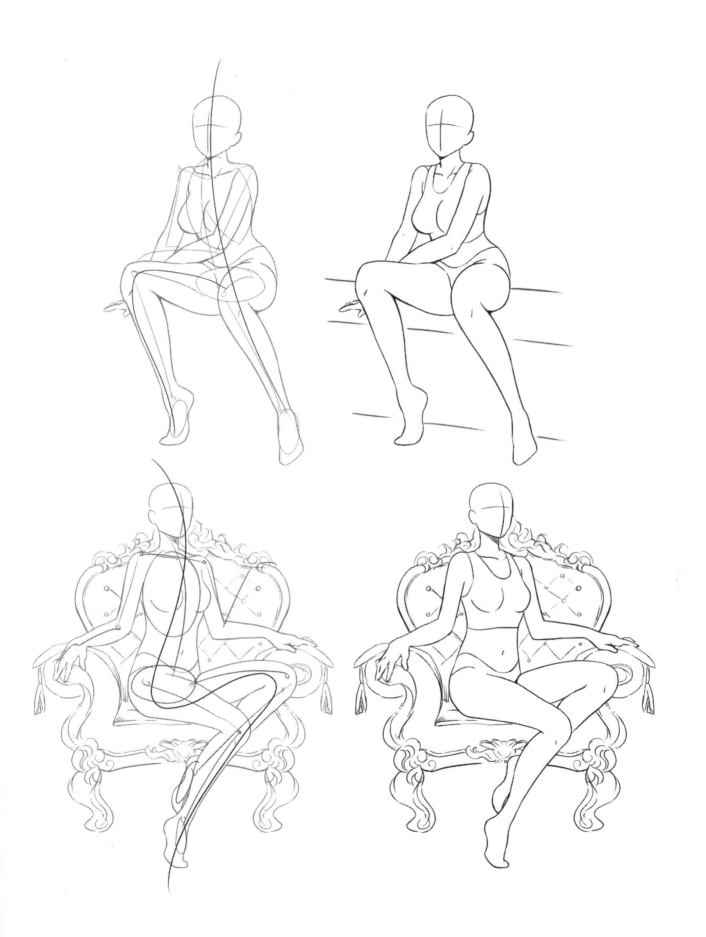

3. Dynamic Poses

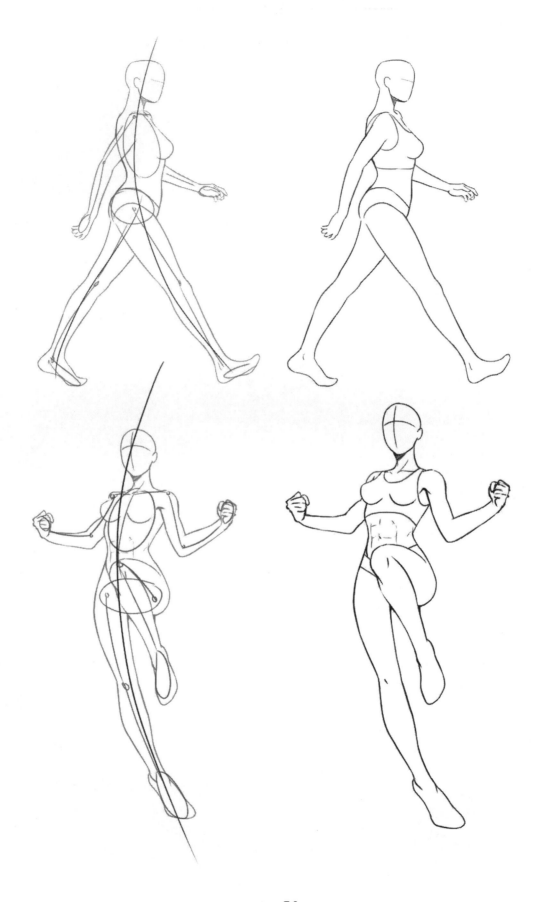

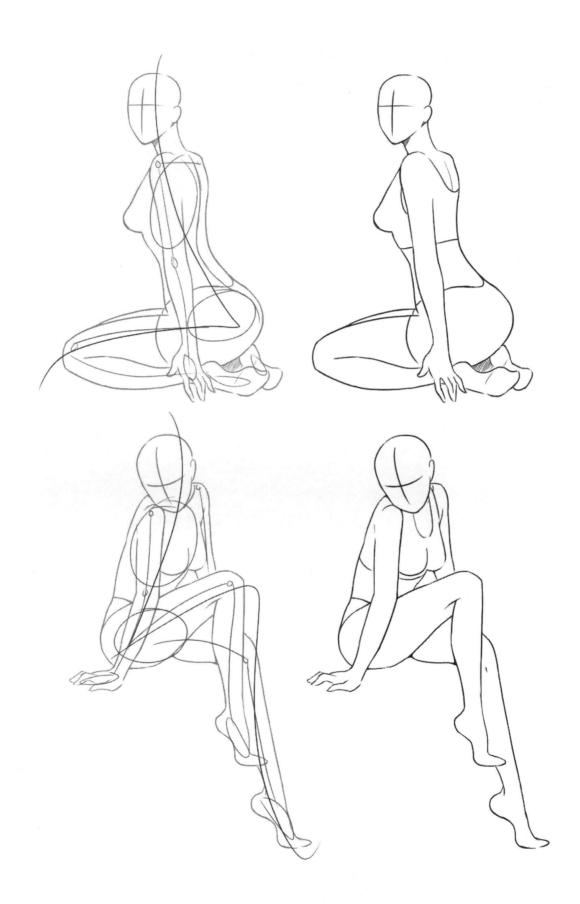

FASHION

Types of Clothing – Materials and Folds

The Materials

Knowing the different types of fabric can help you design the folds and characteristics of each clothing piece. The fabric can be categorized by thickness, texture, softness/rigidness, and gravity.

Soft & Thick

Soft and thick material is heavy so it will be baggy at the bottom. Also, the creases and folds are big.

Stiff & Thick

Similarly, this material is rigid and thick but there are more folds around the elbow where the arm bends.

Soft & Thin

Soft and thin material has the most folds and creases as it wraps around the figure and reveals the organic shape of it.

Stiff & Thin

This is the common dress shirt material where the folds are everywhere.

Pipe Fold

These folds are usually found in dresses or skirts where you see semi-cylindrical or tube-like shapes.

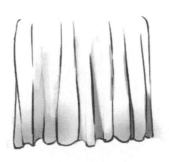

Zigzag Fold

Bunched up fabric that creates diamond-like shapes or triangles that are usually found on the bottom of jeans/pants.

Spiral Fold

Folds created when the material is wrapped around a cylindrical shape like the arms and legs.

Half-lock Fold

This fold occurs when there's a change of direction like on the knees or the middle of the arm.

Drop Fold

This fold is when the material is hanging from a single point, creating the origin of creases.

Diaper Fold

Similar to a drop fold but there are two supports for the diaper fold.

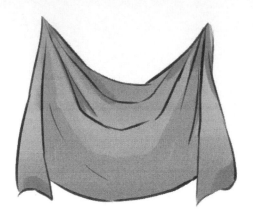

Resting and Turning

When the arm is resting, there will be creases indicating the gravity and the weight of the material. Keep in mind the difference between the soft and stiff material.

When the arm is turning away or twisting, there is a crease motion following the flow.

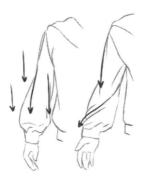

Arm Bending

The elbow becomes the pulling point of the fabric when it bends. Therefore, the materials will stack up more around the bend.

This is where you will find some zigzag or half-lock folds.

Also, following the fold of the arm helps with the rhythm of the folds.

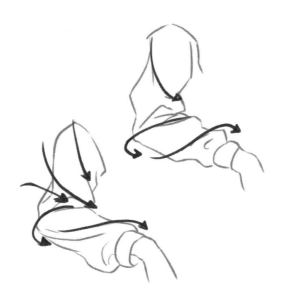

Arm Raising

Think of putting some spiral folds around the raised arm but at an angle and more loosely depending on the material. Make sure they follow the form of the arm.

Bending the Knee

Usually, on the pants, the tension will be on the crotch so it will be the origin of the creases. And then the half-lock fold will just be under the knee.

For a skirt, there will be a stack of creases where the leg bends by the hip. Then the folds will fall around the form of the leg.

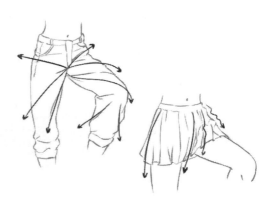

Sitting Down

When sitting down, all the material around the hip will bunch up into spiral folds. For the pants, the tension will always be on the crotch and the knees. However, on the skirt, the flow will continue on the other side while also following gravity.

School Uniforms

Let's learn how to draw a school uniform!

1.   Go ahead and draw a full body character.
2.   Draw the silhouette of the uniform. Don't worry about the folds and wrinkles yet, just focus on following the form of the body.

3.   Determine where most of the wrinkles will happen or where the tension points will be like the underarm, waist, and breasts. There will be fewer folds since this is a stiff, thick material.

The height of the socks will depend on your preference.

4. Add details like the pattern on the pleated skirt and ribbon. Draw the shoes and the bag, too.

Clean up your drawing by erasing the sketch underneath the uniform and you're done!

Other Types of School Uniforms

Long Sleeve with Buttons

Sailor

Sweater on Top

Bolero

With Necktie

Straps

CASUAL OUTFITS

Drawing casual clothing can be overwhelming because of the number of clothing articles to choose from. No worries! We'll go back to the basics then you can use your imagination to mix, match, and even layer them.

1. Choose a pose for your character then decide what type of clothing materials you want.

For this example, we will draw a thin stiff top while the shorts will be thick and stiff like jeans.

We will also draw some boots and a headband.

2. It's better that you plan the type of materials to draw and the folds they will make ahead of actual drawing so that your process will be smooth.

It might help to draw the clothing first like they are stickers or laying on top of a flat surface. Then later you can imagine them as 3-D objects that will wrap around the form of the body.

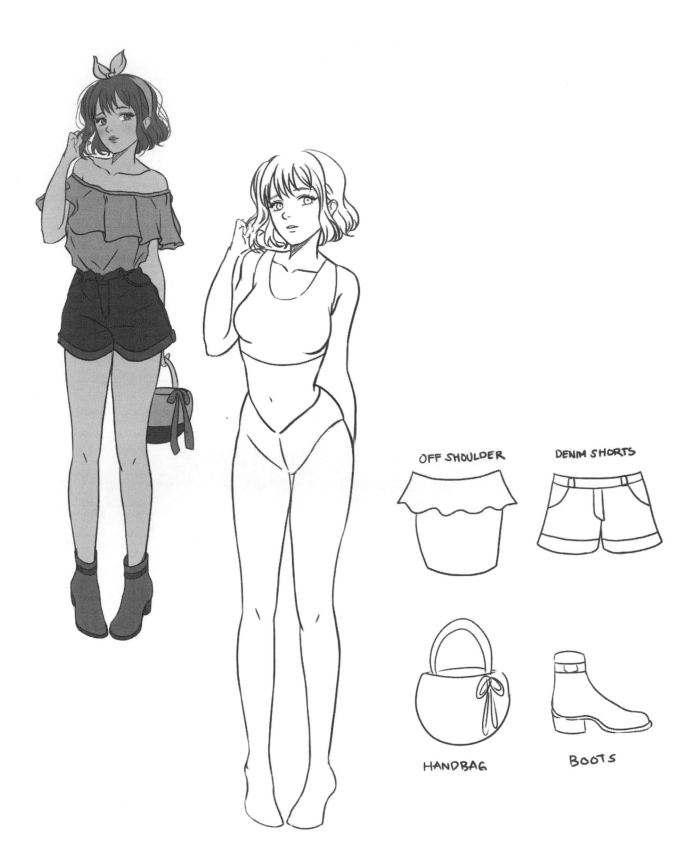

OFF SHOULDER

DENIM SHORTS

HANDBAG

BOOTS

3.   Draw the silhouette around the form.

4. Now that you have the silhouette, it's easier to draw the folds.

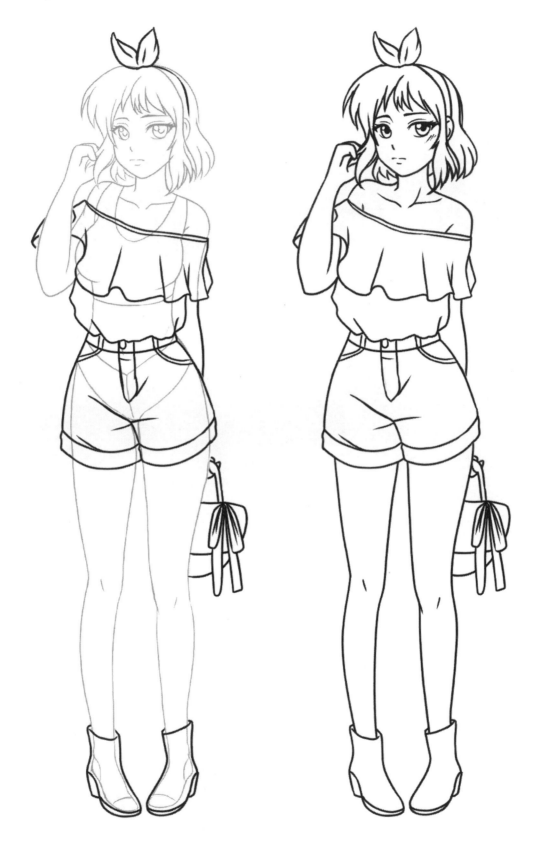

5. Make your lines cleaner then shade your drawing.

Other Examples of Casual Outfits

TRENDY AND DRESSY OUTFITS

Trendy outfits are very fashionable and often are made out of layers of clothing. Now that you know how to draw basic clothes, you can easily layer them on top of each other to create a style that is unique to a character.

1. For this character, we will give her an off-shoulder long-sleeved blouse made from a soft, thick material while her skirt will be a denim material.

We will also add a tied shirt around her hips and tall combat boots to complete the look.

Dark stockings will look fashionable with this outfit.

2. Go ahead and draw these articles of clothing on a flat surface.

3. Let's draw the silhouette around the form of the body.

4. Decide where the main tension points on the clothing will be like the armpit and the breast areas.

5. Add a few more interesting details.

6. Finish up by shading your drawing.

Dressy outfits are categorized as elegant and fancy. They will be simple to draw since we already know how to draw skirts and basic shirts. The key to drawing the puffy skirts is by starting with a cone silhouette.

1. Design a matching hairstyle for this look.
2. Elevate the feet somewhat so it will be easier to draw the heels.
3. The cone will depend on how puffy you want the skirt to be.
4. Just follow the rhythm of the bottom of the feet.

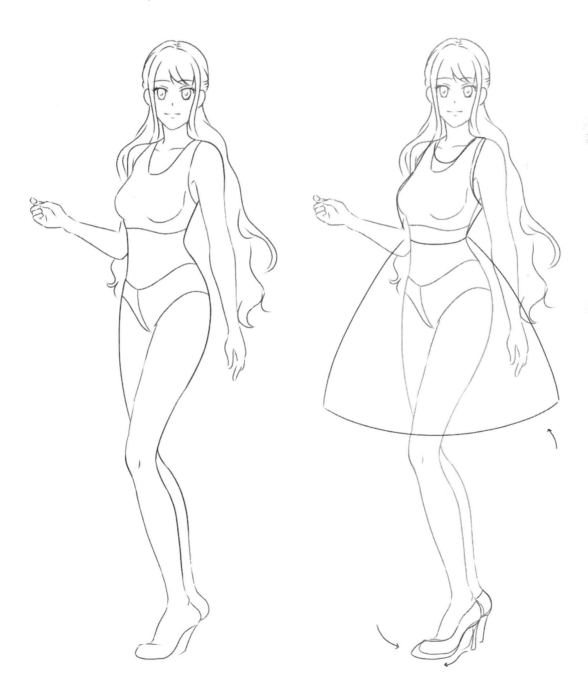

5. The only type of folds you will draw are pipe folds.

6. To draw the ruffles, just draw some random "S" curves.

Make sure they overlap because we will add volume to them on the next step.

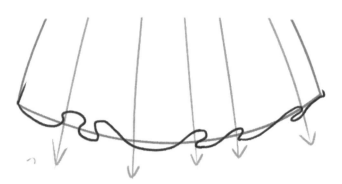

7. Now just add some straight lines following the arrows but put them where there are overlapping folds.

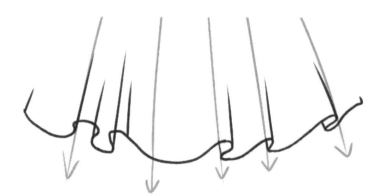

8. Let's add some accessories like some earrings, a necklace, a bracelet, and a handbag.

9. Make a few more adjustments and you're done!

Other Examples of Trendy Outfits

TRADITIONAL OUTFITS

There are a variety of traditional clothing in Japan but we will start by drawing a kimono.

1.   Choose a pose that will showcase the design of the kimono.

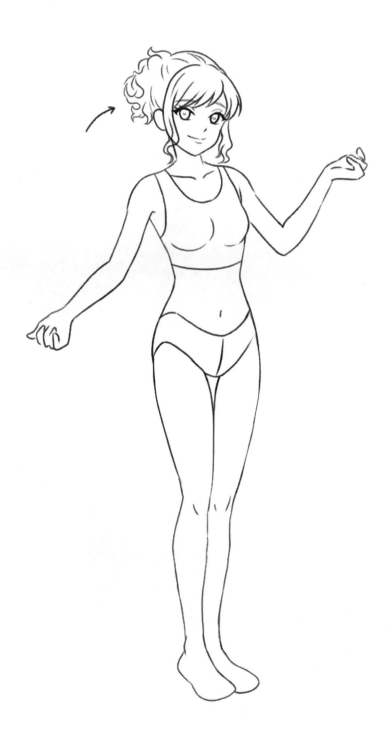

2.   Design the silhouette.

A kimono and a yukata are very similar in appearance. The materials they are made out of differentiate them. A kimono is made of thick material because of the layers of materials underneath while a yukata is mostly made of cotton and worn during warmer weather.

Draw the kimono with fewer creases and double the collar.

3. Add just a few folds, following the flow from the armpits.

120

4. Design the patterns on the kimono. You can use some flowers, stripes, or curvy lines. The limit is your imagination.

Tip: Extravagant patterns are usually for younger women while simpler designs are for older women.

The obi or the belt can have multiple layers, too.

5. Consider adding another accessory like a handbag and you're done!

CHARACTERS

DESIGNING CHARACTERS BY AGE

Facial Features

Body Comparison

Let's go through each body type and compare them to each other.

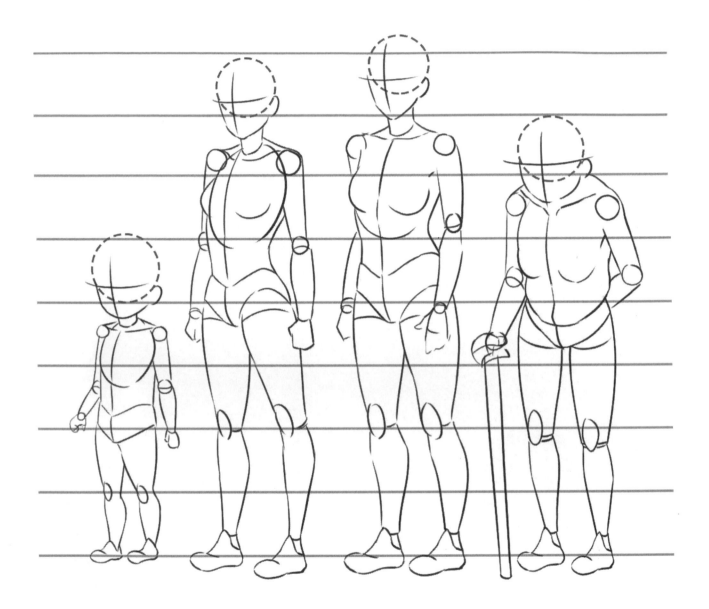

Child

Usually, a child's height is four times the height of the head but it still depends on the age you are drawing.

The younger the child, the fewer heads you will have to multiply. The torso is also quite straight like a rectangle.

Teen

During puberty, a teenage body will develop into a curvier look especially around the hips and the breasts but it will still have a round face.

Adult

An adult woman will have a mature body and face with smaller eyes, etc.

The height and the breasts are more developed compared to a teenager's body.

Senior

For the older lady, her height will be shorter due to the hunching of the back. Typically, she will use a cane to support herself when standing. The curvature on her body like the hips will be replaced by the sagging of the muscles. Therefore, she will appear to have a rounder torso.

The older she gets, the shorter her height will be.

DRAWING A CHILD CHARACTER

1.   Draw a skeleton four times the height of the head. This child will be about 4-6 years old.
2.   Next, draw the rectangular torso and the cylinder limbs. Make sure that the width of the shoulders is not too wide.

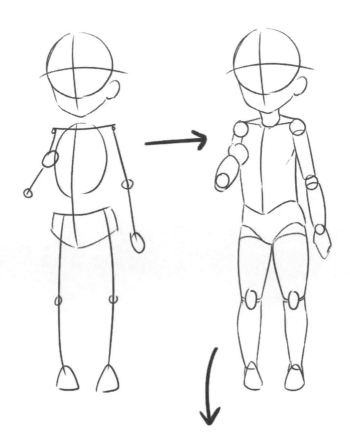

3.   Pick a cute hairstyle like pigtails and a stuffed toy that the child can hold then decide the shape of the eyes.

After that, draw a simple dress.

4.   Choose an expression that will give an innocent, sweet look.

The last step is to add the details and the shading.

Drawing a Teenage Character

The process of drawing a teenage girl is very similar to drawing a child. Start with a skeleton then make a mannequin on top of it. This pose is perfect for her age because it still shows the playfulness that teenagers possess.

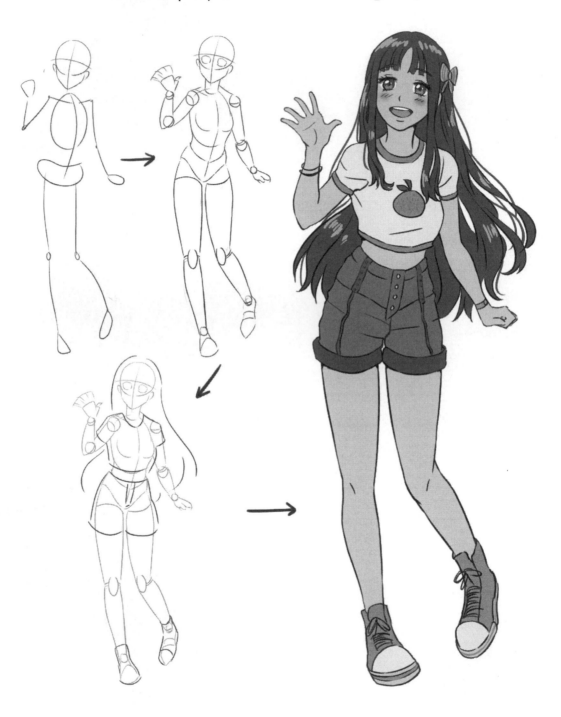

Drawing an Adult Female

For the adult character, draw a stationary, simple pose to indicate the maturity of her age. Draw the skeleton then the mannequin.

Maybe draw a tied-up hairstyle and simple attire like a long loose top, long skirt, and a pair of boots.

Drawing an Older Lady

The older lady may have a hunchback. Therefore, the head and the rib cage will overlap from this angle. From there, draw the mannequin version. Her stomach will also overlap the hip bone.

TYPES OF DERE CHARACTERS

There are many types of "dere" characters in anime. These characters are also known as different personality types. If you want to design a character, knowing these types might help you flesh out your character more.

When drawing a dere type, it's important that we emphasize their personality type using a certain body language and expression. Their choice of clothing and hairstyles are important, too, but it varies in anime, therefore, you don't need to worry too much about them. Let's go through the most common types.

The Tsundere

Tsunderes are not very honest with their feelings because of their pride. They are typically mean and hostile but when they warm up to a person that they like, they will slowly show their cute and sweet side.

1.   Choose a pose that will show her bossy side. The best pose is when she puts her hands on her waist. This really shows a dominant personality. You can also use a pose where she crosses her arms.

Draw the skeleton then the mannequin.

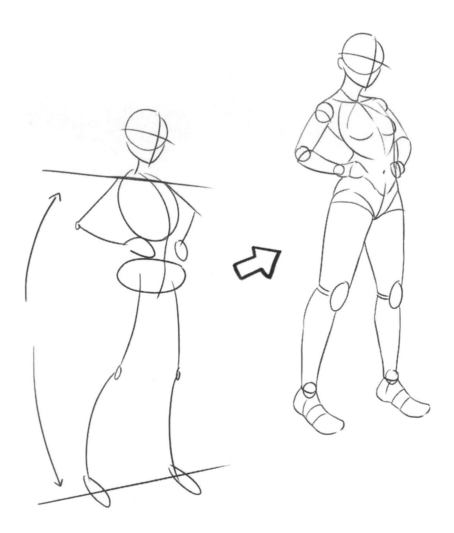

Expression

2.   What really shows is her angry expression because this is the default face.

Make sure to bring the eyebrows closer to her upper eyelids and angle them up-ward. Give her a downside smile, too.

Another thing to remember is to give her sharp eyes. This helps to emphasize her confident personality.

She always has her guard up.

Hairstyle

3.   For a hairstyle, maybe give her a childish hairstyle because this also reflects her sweet side despite putting forth a bold front.

Clothing Style

4.   Lastly, for clothing, put ruffles all over the clothing like the collar, wrists, and socks. Also, make the sleeves puffy.

Even though she's hiding her true personality, her style gives us a glimpse of what she is really all about.

The Yandere

Unlike the tsundere, a yandere is someone who shows her sweet side without a problem. The main difference is that when a yandere loves, she will be very obsessed to the point that she might kill someone who tries to take away her lover. She appears very sweet on the outside but is quite twisted on the inside.

1. Let's choose a pose where she is hiding something behind her. It could be any weapon of your choice. She will use this weapon to carry out her plans with a sinister expression on her face. This pose is also perfect to show her sweet side. Draw the skeleton of this pose then add some volume to make a mannequin.

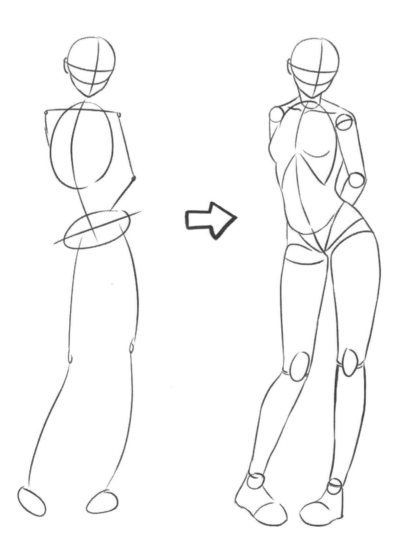

Expression

2.   You can choose the innocent expression or the twisted expression. The innocent expression shows lifted eyebrows and closed smiling eyes while the twisted expression shows the obsession with her character. The eyebrows are also lifted but in a more worried look and the eyes and lips are smiling.

Hairstyle

3.   Any hairstyle that makes her cute is the best option because it hides her true nature well.

For this example, draw parted bangs and a couple of twisted hair buns on the sides.

Clothing Style

4. She is about to commit a crime so wearing something comfortable or easy to move around in will be her choice of clothing.

The same goes for her shoes.

Draw the silhouette on the mannequin sketch.

THE KUUDERE

"Kuu" comes from the word "cool" and "dere" means love-stuck. So, Kuuderes are very emotionless. Nothing seems to affect them except when they fall in love because they will start showing their cute side to the lucky person. Other than that, they are very frank and don't hold back their thoughts and opinions.

1. Kuuderes are very simple in nature so a simple pose will be enough to express their personality. Start off with a good gesture of the skeleton then proceed with the shapes of the human figure.

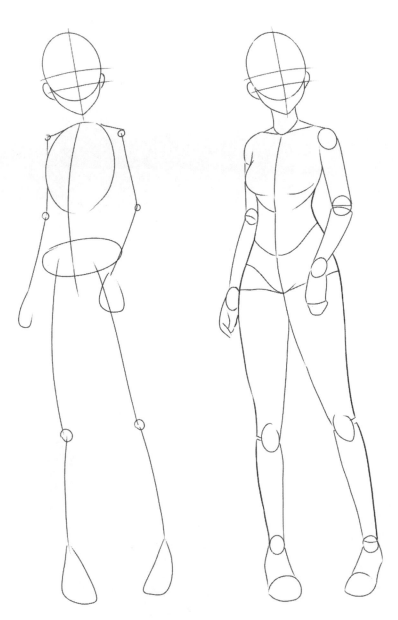

Expression

2.   To make an expressionless face, all you have to do is draw the eyebrows and lips as straight lines.

Hairstyle

3.   This hairstyle has one-sided swept bangs and a long ponytail.

Draw the silhouette first then add the details.

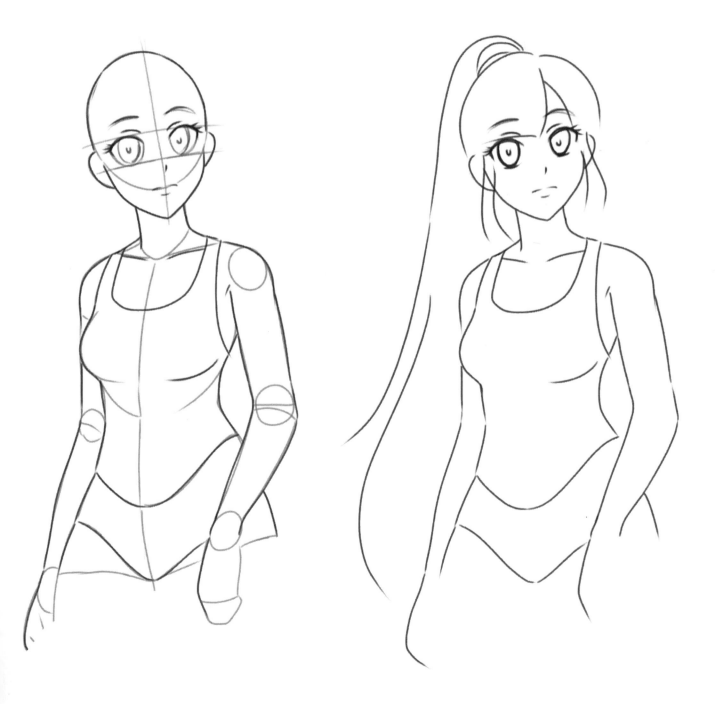

Clothing Style

4. Her clothing is made out of soft material and is quite fit around the arms. Make sure to draw many folds here. The skirt is parted into three sections.

Give her some boots and a collar and you're done!

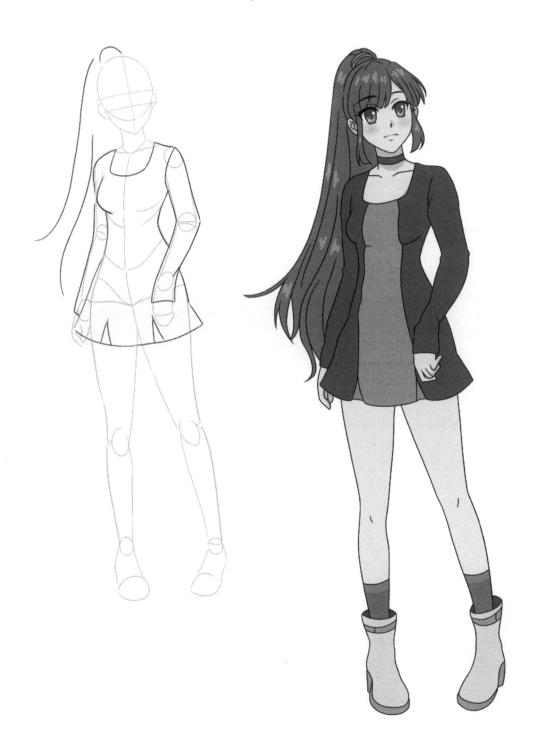

THE DEREDERE

Derederes are the most extrovert among the dere types. They spread positivity around because they are full of joy and energy. You will definitely notice if something is wrong when they aren't cheerful.

1.   Pick a pose that shows her energy from top to bottom. The pose that we will draw looks like she is in the middle of a jump. She's fired up to give her best again. Follow that curved rhythm from the top of her head to her toes.

Expression

2.   For her eyes, make them as round as you can but the bottom should be curved up a little because she is smiling widely. This causes her cheeks to lift under her eyes.

Also, note the lifted eyebrows.

Hairstyle

3.   This pigtail hairstyle not only reflects her childish personality but also her high spirits as they are drawn high on her head.

Clothing Style

4. Since she is a childish deredere, we will give her lots of layered ruffles and a cute pair of shoes.

Being a deredere is not limited to childish characters. You can still design them as adults but make sure their style mirrors their age.

THE DANDERE

Danderes are quite similar to kuuderes because they sometimes don't have emotions shown on their faces. The big difference is that danderes are often quiet because they are too shy to talk. They only talk if you talk to them directly and are typically shy or embarrassed. Kuuderes may be able to keep their cool even when they're *embarrassed but danderes can't.*

1. Since danderes are extremely shy, use the arms to make a barrier between them and the people they are talking to. This is how shy people subconsciously show their body language. Bring both hands to their chest.

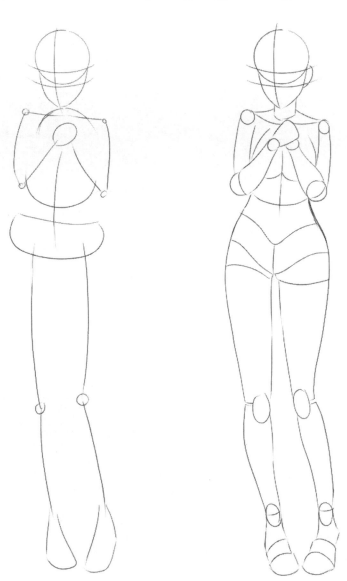

Expression

2. Let's draw an expression where she is trying her best to talk while being flustered.

The eyebrows are worried and her mouth is slightly open because she talks very quietly. She will also blush a lot.

Hairstyle

3. Her hairstyle is a bit curly and short. The bangs are one-sided and swept behind her ear.

She subconsciously tucks behind this hair just to hide her embarrassment.

Clothing Style

4.   Since she has an adorable personality at her core, try to mirror this by giving her a cute and simple dress.

After that, just add the details on her hair and her clothing then you're done!

CHARACTERS FROM A FANTASY WORLD

Fantasy characters are going to be more detailed and aesthetic than the previous characters that we've drawn *but the process is fairly simple* because we will go through everything in small steps.

The overall method is similar to the previous characters. We start with the gesture of the skeleton then the mannequin or the figure. Next we will draw the expression and the hairstyle as well as the clothing that suits our character. Lastly, we will polish up the details.

We will just have to spend more time designing the characters' clothing *because* the pieces *can be quite detailed.*

THE FEMALE KNIGHT

One of the most important things to do first before sketching your character is to envision their personality type. For a knight, she will be reserved. We want to emit her powerful aura through her pose and clothing. Since she has trained a lot to be a knight, her body would be developed like an athlete or maybe even more fit.

1.   We want a pose that will showcase her sword but also show us her composed personality at the same time.

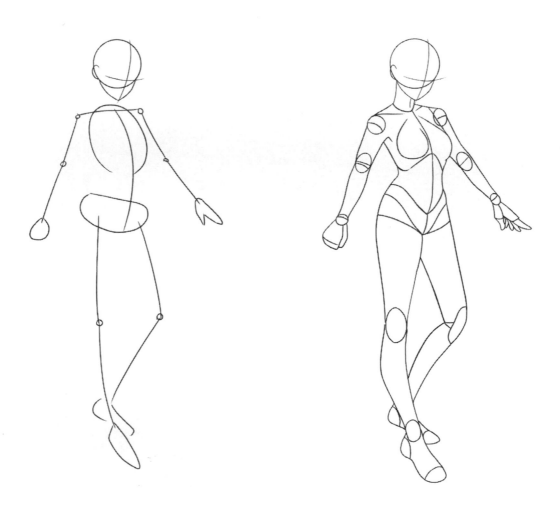

Expression

2. Give her a fierce gaze since we know that she is a resilient and brave character.

Her eyebrows are closer to her inner eyes and her lips are tight.

Hairstyle

3. Her hairstyle will be a ponytail because she doesn't want her hair to get in the way of fighting.

We also want the hair to be flowing because of the wind. To do this, draw some random "S" curves but remember that the volume closer to her head will be heavy compared to the ends of the hair.

Armor Design

4.   Her body will be covered in armor like the shoulders, upper torso, forearms, and lower legs. It can be intimidating to design the armor but if you look closely, each piece of armor starts from basic shapes.

Her torso and shoulder armor just looks like a basic t-shirt while the forearm guards look like rectangular shapes that wrap around the form of the arms.

The same thing applies to the lower legs and knees.

Repeating Patterns

5.   Now that we have the basic foundation, drawing some details on top will be easy. Think of a pattern that you want to design on her armor. It can be as simple or as complicated as you want but the basic idea is to use this pattern all over the armor to get a harmonized design.

For example, we want to use some pointy leafy shapes, spirals, and diamonds on her. This could be an emblem of her kingdom as well.

You can see this pattern on her shoulder, breastplate, arms, and knees. The result gives us an appealing design. Notice also that the armor has more details like some lines that follow the form of the body and pointy shapes that reflect her personality.

Clothing Design

6.   Drawing what's underneath the armor will be much easier now. Draw a collar and some gloves that reach her upper arms. Her skirt is made out of individual leather pieces so they each can move freely.

There are also a few more layers of cloth that wrap around her waist. Since there is a gust of wind, these fabrics will sway.

Weapon Design

7.   Just like her armor, her sword will also have the same pattern of diamonds, spirals, and pointy curves.

KNIGHT – COMPLETED DRAWING

THE PRINCESS

A princess is elegant even when moving in small gestures. We will capture this through her pose. Draw a simple standing pose with her arms showing elegance and royalty. She will be wearing a ballgown with different layers and intricate designs.

1.   Her personality is mature as it is necessary due to her role as the princess.

Her arms are raised gracefully and her head is slightly tilted to the side.

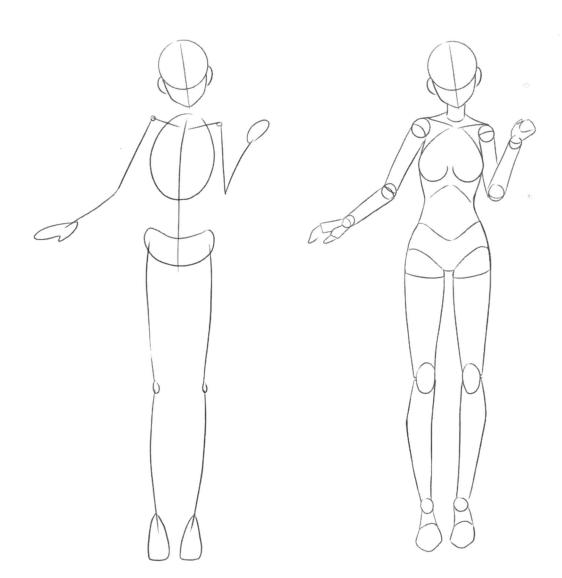

Expression

2.   Her expression is just a simple smile. She is very reserved.

Hairstyle

3.   You may choose to give her an updo hairstyle but for our princess here, she will have long, wavy hair. It will be short in the front but long at the back.

Later, we will give her lots of accessories like flower ornaments and a small crown.

Gown Foundation

4.   A ballgown takes up a lot of space but overall, the shape is simple. It is just a cone that starts from the waist while the top part is shaped like a heart.

Make sure that the edge of the skirt is touching the ground.

Shape Design

5.   We've covered the largest shape which is the foundation. Now we will do the medium shapes. This shape looks like a butterfly and is perfect for framing her head.

This will guide the eyes to her face.

This gown is layered with many types of materials from thin to thick.

We don't need to concerned about the layers under-neath.

Accessories

6. Draw some flowers and a small crown behind her side bangs. Her gloves are only covering her forearms and have some ruffles at the border.

Her collar might look complicated but it comes from a basic shape of a cylinder and a bent rectangle.

Repeating Patterns

7. It's time to add the small details. Draw the butterfly shape into wavy lines to turn into ruffles. The "V" shape on her chest will have the same pattern as the knight's armor but it will be more detailed.

Also, draw another layer of thin material around her waist and make it short.

These trims of the butterfly shape will have a repeating pattern of random curves. It doesn't have to be fully de-tailed because the embroidery will have the same color as the fabric.

Lastly, the bottom of the gown will show the layers underneath that made the gown look puffy.

PRINCESS – COMPLETED DRAWING

THE ANGEL

1.   Let's draw a flying angel that is coming down from the sky and imagine that
     we are looking up at her. The wind will blow her hair and clothing just like
     the knight example. This angle is ideal to show her great power as an angel.

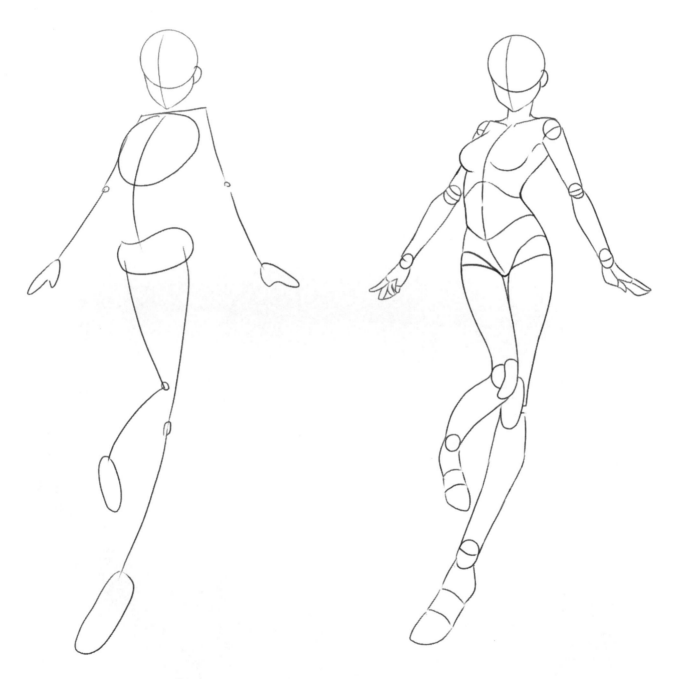

Expression & Hairstyle

2.   A neutral expression will be enough for her but draw her hair using "S"
     curves as a base.

Clothing Foundation

3. Draw a simple rectangular top and a very wide belt around her hips. This belt is where the loose fabrics will attach.

To make it look like that they are floating, draw some "S" curves just like when drawing the hair. Since this fabric is light and thin, it will create a lot of folds and creases.

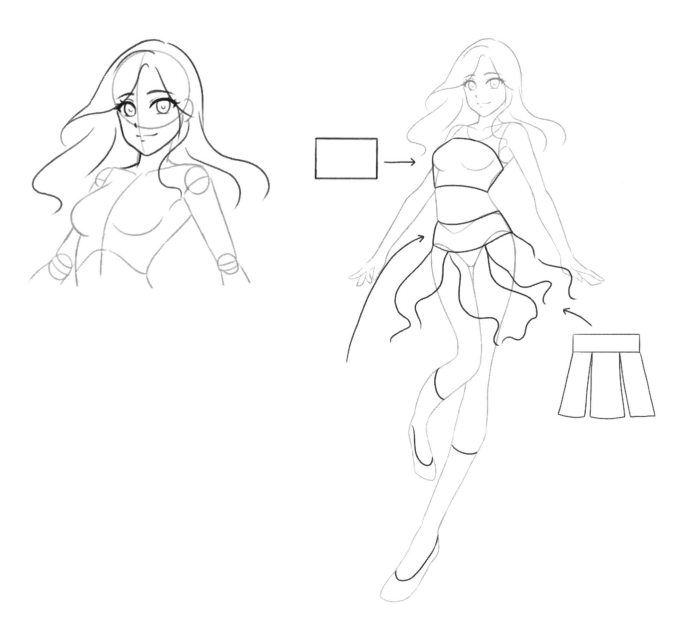

Repeating Patterns

4. What pattern or shapes would you like to design on her clothing? Let's use a diamond shape and wings as the repeating pattern.

This wing design is easy to draw. It starts off looking like a mango and then you just add the three individual feathers. Draw this shape on her head and on the sides of her shoes.

For other areas like the arms and legs, draw some strings that create "X" shapes.

Wings Foundation

5. Let's design some wings. After all, what is an angel without wings? Wings are mostly drawn using triangle shapes as the base.

This will depend on the angle of the wings.

The ones we will draw show her flapping since our angel is coming down.

After you have the triangle base, draw some layered feathers. You don't need to draw each feather because it might be too distracting to the viewer.

We want the attention to her face, not her wings.

From the top of the wings, the feathers are very short and they get progressively longer as you go down the layers.

ANGEL – COMPLETED DRAWING

THE ELF

Elves are known for their grace and agility. Not only can they use magic but they can also master weapons such as a bow and arrow. Let's pick a pose that will capture her grace and beauty.

1. Draw an elf that is in the middle of attacking with her bow and arrow. Her right arm is drawing the bowstring close to her face, therefore, her left arm would be straight as it holds the tension of the bow.

Expression

2.   Her expression will be very focused as she is trying to shoot her target. Her eyes and eyebrows will look like they are angry because of squinting but to balance this, give her a smirk.

Since she is an elf, make sure to give her pointy ears. This gives her the advantage to hear things that humans don't normally hear.

Hairstyle

3.   For the hairstyle, let's draw very long twisted hair. This will add grace to her movements and overall look.

Elves are also known to live for thousands of years so adding long hair will give hints of her ancient days.

Clothing Foundation

4. The base of her costume is a t-shirt with puffy sleeves and tight-fitting pants. She will also have arm guards on her forearms and knee-high boots.

Draw a quiver where she will store her arrow supply.

It will not be visible from this angle but the belt strap will wrap around her chest.

Repeating Patterns

5. Next, draw a corset on her and additional protection of thick cloth around her waist.

The repeating pattern is a series of "X" lines that can be added to the arm guards, the side of her pants, and her shirt.

Bow & Arrow Design

6.   We already know that a bow looks like a "C" but it gets curvier when it is being pulled and stretched.

The overall shape of the bow is based on a very wide slice of pizza.

When looking at the bow like this, we can see that the base shape looks like an upper lip.

Once you have this as a base, you can design it however you want.

The arrow should be in-between her index and middle finger while the rest of her fingers are drawing the strings.

And don't forget to add a few more arrows in her quiver.

ELF – COMPLETED DRAWING

THE MAID

1. The maid that we will draw is a tireless maid because she is too busy serving her Highness with everything she desires. She will be serving some tea to her Majesty so let's draw her right hand holding a tray full of teacups. Her left arm will be holding the teapot.

Expression & Hairstyle

2.   Her expression will be neutral as she is trying to remain professional during working hours while her hair will be neat and tied up in pigtails.

Clothing Foundation

3.   The foundation of her uniform is a simple dress with long sleeves that are puffy around the shoulders. The cuffs are long, too.

Additional Details

4.   Draw some ruffles as a headband and a collar. You can also draw more ruffles for the trim on her dress.

Then add an apron as well as a ribbon on the back of her dress.

Props

5.   The last thing to do is draw the tray of teacups and the teapot then you're done!

Maid – Completed Drawing

Conclusion

Drawing anime is pretty simple, isn't it? Now you understand the foundation of how everything works.

Let's go over what we've learned so far. First, we learned how to draw the head from different angles and then how to draw and stylize the facial features like the eyes, nose, and mouth. Next, we learned about hair and how to draw it from a silhouette to the sections and to add details as well as the different body types and how to draw them from varied angles and poses.

After that, we learned the logic behind the folds and creases on a wide variety of clothing materials and saw how it was affected when worn in certain poses. Lastly, we drew characters of different ages, identified specific dere types, and experimented with a variety of fantasy characters to offer inspiration to create your own characters.

In anime, the drawing style might differ from person to person but that's only because the proportions are tweaked. So have fun experimenting with what really suits your preference. After all, learning to draw from others is like trying out different recipes; we experiment with recipes and adjust them according to our desired tastes.

Additionally, if you practice every day, it will lead to steady improvement. You might not see a difference within a day or two, but you will see improvement over time. You can start by drawing the head and keep adding details as you proceed through the book. The key is not to try everything at once because it most likely will overwhelm you, but rather add bits and pieces to slowly build and sharpen your confidence and skills.

I hope that this book will help you on your art journey to achieve the level that you dream of. So what are you waiting for? It's time to grab a pencil and start drawing!

Thank you for getting our book!

If you find this drawing book fun and useful, we would be very grateful if you post a short review on Amazon! Your support does make a difference and we read every review personally.

If you would like to leave a review, just head on over to this book's Amazon page and click "Write a customer review".

Thank you for your support!

Printed in Great Britain
by Amazon